"They're All
Writers"

"They're All Writers"

TEACHING PEER TUTORING IN THE ELEMENTARY WRITING CENTER

Jennifer Sanders
Rebecca L. Damron

TEACHERS COLLEGE PRESS

TEACHERS COLLEGE | COLUMBIA UNIVERSITY
NEW YORK AND LONDON

NATIONAL WRITING PROJECT
BERKELEY, CA

Published simultaneously by Teachers College Press, 1234 Amsterdam Avenue, New York, NY 10027 and National Writing Project, 2105 Bancroft Way, Berkeley, CA 94720-1042.

Through its mission, the National Writing Project (NWP) focuses the knowledge, expertise, and leadership of our nation's educators on sustained efforts to help youth become successful writers and learners. NWP works in partnership with local Writing Project sites, located on nearly 200 university and college campuses, to provide high-quality professional development in schools, universities, libraries, museums, and after-school programs. NWP envisions a future where every person is an accomplished writer, engaged learner, and active participant in a digital, interconnected world.

Library of Congress Cataloging-in-Publication Data

Names: Sanders, Jennifer, 1976 author. | Damron, Rebecca L., author.
Title: "They're all writers" : teaching peer tutoring in the elementary writing
   center / Jennifer Sanders, Rebecca Damron.
Description: New York : Teachers College Press, 2017. | Includes bibliographical
   references and index.
Identifiers: LCCN 2016049530 (print) | LCCN 2016056003 (ebook) |
   ISBN 9780807758205 (pbk. : alk. paper) | ISBN 9780807775608 (ebook)
Subjects: LCSH: Peer teaching. | Tutors and tutoring. | Writing centers. |
   Language arts (Elementary)
Classification: LCC LB1031.5 .S26 2017 (print) | LCC LB1031.5 (ebook) |
   DDC 372.62/3—dc23
LC record available at https://lccn.loc.gov/2016049530

ISBN 978-0-8077-5820-5 (paper)
ISBN 978-0-8077-7560-8 (ebook)

Printed on acid-free paper
Manufactured in the United States of America

24   23   22   21   20   19   18   17   8   7   6   5   4   3   2   1

Contents

Acknowledgments

Many people have contributed to this work in many ways. Chapter 2 was cowritten with Dr. Sheri Vasinda, a colleague at Oklahoma State University. Her expertise and perspectives have been invaluable, and we thank her for contributing to this work. Several OSU English graduate students assisted us with designing the initial writing center peer tutoring lessons, collecting research data, and writing reflections on their experiences with the project: Karen Chavira, Shawn Chiusano, Melody Denny, Kim Dyer, Caroline Fisher, John Hansen, Brianna Hooks, Elijah Johnson, LuElla Putnam, and Catelyn Vasquez. A cadre of wonderful classroom teachers worked with us to teach the writing center peer tutoring lessons to their students, organize and run the writing centers, revise and strengthen the tutor training lessons, and write reflections on the implementation of the lessons. Jan Anderson, Heather Corbett, Julie Farrington, Meghan Griffith, Carey Henderson, Quincy Hunt, Jason Harrison, Jackie Iob, Amanda Milinkovich, Angel Muzik, Megan Ools, Annie Ortiz, and Cate Pogue: without you all, this idea would have never grown into such powerful practice. Heather Corbett passed away in late 2012 as a result of cancer. Her passion was contagious, and her commitment to this project was invaluable. She was an excellent, amazing teacher, and we dedicate this work to her and the legacy of all great teachers.

Writing Centers in the Elementary School

When most elementary school educators hear the term *writing center*, they visualize a classroom space stocked with lined, unlined, and colored papers; a variety of markers, pens, and pencils; and other materials children would use in independent writing. However, when the educators involved in this project began designing our first writing center, the type of space we had in mind resembled a university writing center where students bring their writing for peer tutoring focused on that piece of writing. The idea of a student-led writing center for peer tutoring was born from long-term collaboration and colearning, facilitated by our National Writing Project site at Oklahoma State University. Annie Ortiz, a 4th-grade teacher and OSU Writing Project codirector, was one of our partners in this work. Below, we open with her story about noticing the needs of her students for greater responsibility and agency in their work and the realization that a writing center could meet the teachers' and students' needs.

In this book, we share what we have developed and learned from these collaborations—from the germination of an idea to the development of a writing center and peer tutoring curriculum; from our exploration into possible models and structures for a writing center to our research and reflection on student learning. At the risk of sounding like an infomercial, we have included in this book all the essential components a teacher would need to establish a writing center and teach students how to be effective writing peer tutors. Over the course of several years, these lessons have been taught with students across the range of elementary grade levels, and the resulting student (and teacher) learning has been invigorating.

Although student-led writing centers have been present in American universities since the 1930s (Carino, 1995; Murphy & Law, 1995) and are quite popular as a means of improving writing

1

at the high school level, their presence in elementary schools is extremely rare. In fact, some elementary writing educators argue that peer conferencing, the essence of writing center interactions, is difficult to implement productively in elementary classrooms because of the metacognitive skills required. They also predict that peer conferences may be limited to editing tasks and conversations about the writing process rather than the rich development of the writing content (Fletcher, Portalupi, & Williams, 2006; Routman, 2000). However, through this work, we have learned that peer conferencing and peer tutoring are viable at the elementary level and can lead to collaborative learning whereby both parties grow as writers from the interaction. Bruffee (1984) states, and we agree, that "the way [writers] talk with each other determines the way they will think and the way they will write" (quoted in Villanueva, 2003, p. 422). Conversations between writers can be powerful sites of learning about writing.

A PERCOLATING IDEA:
HOW SKYLINE ELEMENTARY GOT ITS WRITING CENTER

When I was little, my parents began their day with steaming cups of coffee. They had an old silver coffee pot with a metal filter that would sit down inside the pot. You would fill the pot with water, drop in the filter, and spoon in deep-brown coffee. A small lid with a little clear top covered it all. As the coffee percolated it would bubble and bubble. You could see, hear, and smell when the coffee was ready for the cup.

My thinking is like that coffee pot. I percolate on ideas. Stuff them in, let them sit, and then they bubble to the point of being ready for the next step. That's how the writing center at Skyline began. In February, after the 5th-graders at my school had completed the state writing test, their teachers looked bedraggled. They said they didn't really know how to teach writing. I understood that frustration and tucked the thought away.

Later, as the year wound down and the hormones of 5th-graders were popping up, frustration lingered in the air. The art teacher asked 5th-graders what they needed. They replied, "More responsibility." I thought, "Of course they do; they need to give back." It was their last year of elementary school. I tucked that tidbit away along with the teacher's frustration at teaching writing. I started percolating.

I knew the OSU (Oklahoma State University) Writing Project's Summer Institute was around the corner and writing ideas would be bountiful. I wondered what I could glean from this summer. As the institute opened, a fellow participant introduced herself as a tutor for a writing center at another university. Her fervor about the writing center was ever present. I heard her, all 5 weeks of the institute, give voice to this passion. Frustration and passion didn't seem a recipe for good coffee, but the ideas were still percolating.

During the last week of the Summer Institute, the director of OSU's writing center, Rebecca Damron, was a guest speaker. She described what the writing center was, how it helped incoming freshmen, who worked there, how they liked to team with high schools, and a variety of ways professors got their students to the writing center. All of a sudden my percolating ideas bubbled over. The coffee was ready. I was about to burst out of my seat.

During lunch break, I went down to the writing center. There was Rebecca talking to Britton, the then-director of our Writing Project. I wondered aloud, *"So do you think you could start a writing center in an elementary school?"* I knew it would give 5th-grade teachers knowledge about writing and give 5th-grade students responsibility, and there would be a definite love of writing spilling over from dedicated tutors. If you wanted to get students to a writing center, the place to start was in an elementary school. I unveiled those sentiments to Rebecca. "Well, why not?" was her response.

And that's how Skyline Elementary got its writing center. A few percolating ideas brewed together to make one steaming success. This is our recipe. We like the rich flavor and want to share. Try it. See how its tastes for you. Add some cream, honey, sugar, or vanilla. Tweak the recipe and find your own way to strengthen the brew.

Annie Ortiz, 4th-grade teacher,
Oklahoma State University Writing Project codirector

PEER TUTORING LESSONS

Before we could open the writing center and send students off to tutor one another in writing, we needed to teach them how to talk about writing and how to coach another writer in improving his or her piece. We designed a series of eight lessons to teach children essential components of writing—such as clear ideas and content, organization, and effective word choice—and to teach them ways to talk about writing and the writing process with peers. English graduate students who were tutors in the university's writing center helped us create and teach these writing lessons to the 5th-grade students at Skyline Elementary. The lessons were taught once a week over the course of 8 weeks and lasted about an hour each. There were four 5th-grade classrooms, taught by Heather Corbett, Julie Farrington, Carey Henderson, and Cate Pogue. Some of the 5th-grade teachers chose to lead a review after the lessons in order to emphasize the main ideas. The teachers usually conducted a second lesson during the week, in between visits from the OSU writing center tutors. This second lesson would either be a follow-up to the weekly tutor training lesson or a time for students to draft a piece of writing in preparation for the upcoming lesson. The lessons evolved over a period of 4 years into the following process:

Week 1: Metaphors for the Writing Process
Week 2: Learning to Peer Tutor with the WRITE mnemonic
Week 3: Peer Tutoring Skit
Week 4: Ideas and Content—"Show, Don't Tell"
Week 5: Organization
Week 6: Word Choice and Sentence Fluency
Week 7: Conventions
Week 8: Practice Peer Tutoring

These tutor training lessons are detailed in Chapter 6. The final versions of the lessons were heavily revised by both us and the 4th- and 5th-grade teachers based on trial and error with the initial lessons and on what we felt was important. Therefore, these lessons have been vetted in real classrooms multiple times. We hope that you will try them out in your own classrooms and modify and adapt the lessons to fit your needs and the students you teach. We'd love to hear the lessons you develop and the modifications you make!

THE SKYLINE WRITING CENTER

The Skyline Writing Center opened in January 2011 and was in operation until the beginning of May. The teachers decided that the best location for the writing center (WC) would be in the school library/media center. The WC was open for peer tutoring once a week, at the same time each week, for about 45 minutes and staffed by two or three university writing tutors. We started small, with just the 4th- and 5th-grade classes. We knew these teachers were excited about the writing center and invested in making it work. The 5th-graders tutored the 4th-graders. Fifth graders were called "coaches" or tutors, and 4th-graders were called the "creators" or writers. Fifth-graders volunteered to tutor each week and were paired up with a 4th-grader who had signed up requesting to come to the Writing Center. The adult facilitators were in charge of assigning a "creator" to a particular "coach" and providing assistance to the 5th-graders when the conversations stalled. Although this model was not without its challenges, we were able to establish a writing center that created space for some amazing conversations and writing to happen. We have woven classroom teachers' stories and insights into the process of implementing a peer tutoring writing center in an elementary school in certain chapters so that readers can hear the teachers' firsthand experiences.

It is important for us to describe the student populations with whom we were working. Skyline Elementary serves a largely low-income community of families. At the time of this writing, approximately 57% of the students received free or reduced price meals. Seventy-five percent of the student population was Caucasian, with the other 25% being a balanced mix of African American, Hispanic, and Native American ethnicities. The population was from mostly working-class White backgrounds, and this was a high-needs demographic. Similarly, the second school we worked with, Will Rogers Elementary, served a low-income community: Eighty-one percent of the students received free or reduced-price meals; 63% of the population was Caucasian and 17% was Hispanic. The remaining 20% were Native American (7%), African American (7%), Asian (4%), and students of other ethnicities (2%). The students leading these peer tutoring sessions were diverse and typically from meager means. Some were students who were often seen in the nurse's office, the principal's office, or sitting in the hallway, because they were "in trouble." Yet, as Annie Ortiz so wisely inferred, they needed and craved responsibility and respect and were willing to work hard to achieve these needs.

POWERFUL PRACTICE IS CONTAGIOUS:
THE WILL ROGERS WRITING CENTER

National Writing Project community members teach each other and ignite sparks of excitement in one another for teaching writing. We,

Jenn and Rebecca, presented our work with Skyline's Writing Center at Oklahoma State University's Writing Project Summer Institute, and Jackie Iob, a reading specialist at Will Rogers Elementary, was one of the summer scholars attending the institute. She said, "I'm really interested in starting a writing center at my school! Can you come and talk to the teachers about this work?" Of course, we enthusiastically said yes. We met with several teachers at Will Rogers, and after a few conversations about the possibilities, a 4th-grade teacher and the three 5th-grade teachers decided to start a writing center.

The writing center at Will Rogers was structured and managed differently from the one at Skyline. The teachers decided to house the writing centers in their classrooms—one in a 4th-grade room and one in a 5th-grade room. They opened the center up to writers from Grades 1 through 4 to attend. The following year, two brand-new, first-year 4th- and 5th-grade teachers directed the writing center and taught the peer tutoring lessons for a second iteration of the writing center at Will Rogers. In Chapter 4, we discuss different structures of the writing centers as well as the logistics of establishing, maintaining, and sustaining an elementary school writing center. We share ideas for gaining support from administrators for the writing center and offer suggestions for negotiating the work needed to sustain the writing center.

When working with the teachers and students, we quickly realized that they needed easy access to all the materials—the lesson plans and tutoring charts used in training the writing tutors. Their need for access to these materials was the impetus for this book. Detailed lesson plans make up Chapter 6, and tutoring charts are located at the end of that chapter. Appendix A contains supporting materials for the tutor training lessons as well as lesson options for the lower elementary grades for the first, introductory lesson. Unlike the Skyline Project in which OSU college students worked with teachers to implement the tutor training lessons, teachers at Will Rogers Elementary took the lead and implemented most of the lessons on their own, with Jenn occasionally coteaching a lesson here or there. This book contains the materials and information you need to teach your students how to peer tutor and to get a writing center up and running at your school.

DOCUMENTING STUDENT LEARNING

Jenn's research expertise is in qualitative literacy research in educational settings, and Rebecca's research expertise is in discourse analysis, so our interests came together perfectly in the decision to focus on the students' peer tutoring conversations while they were in the writing center. We collected research data on the writing center tutoring sessions and interactions with the following questions in mind:

- What types of conversations take place in the tutoring sessions of an elementary school writing center?
- What types of knowledge about writing are constructed during students' writing center conversations?

We wanted to know what students talked about during the peer tutoring sessions, the types of dialogue that took place, and what children were learning about writing. We interviewed students at various points in the year, audio-recorded 18 peer tutoring sessions, and collected observational data during the sessions. In Chapter 5, we dwell in the wonder of child talk. We share excerpts from the children's tutoring sessions, identify and describe the types of conversations they had, and highlight the deep and synthetic learning that took place. We also share our ideas (based on the research data) about what makes a tutoring session more or less successful and how teachers can guide students during the tutoring sessions to provide support, when needed, that enriches student dialogues.

OUR GOALS FOR THIS BOOK

Too many elementary school teachers don't teach writing. They may be hesitant about their own abilities as writers, they may have had bad experiences with writing in their past, or they may have had little or no preparation in writing pedagogy in their teacher education programs. Given teachers' concerns or lack of experience with writing and writing pedagogy, many teachers are anxious about the Common Core State Standards (CCSS) or their state's respective standards and the new emphasis on writing instruction in the elementary literacy curriculum. The CCSS brought writing instruction to a place of prominence (rightfully so), and many teachers need support in developing a writing curriculum that is both effective and manageable and that meets the CCSS or other state standards. While the writing workshop has been demonstrated to be an effective instructional approach, many teachers are intimidated by the complexity of running a successful writing workshop. We fully believe in workshop and process approaches to writing, but we also believe that teachers need options. The writing center approach incorporates the writing process differently and provides a new option for elementary writing teachers. However, it also pairs well with workshop approaches to writing instruction. Our writing center and peer coaching model may also offer new ideas for teachers who are already employing workshop methods in their classrooms.

This book is designed to provide elementary classroom teachers with the background knowledge and practical instructional materials needed to implement a writing center curriculum. The lessons and ideas included here could be easily applied at the middle school level as well. Chapter 2 provides foundational information about writing process theory and practice. Theory is a teacher's touchstone: Knowledge of the theory behind our practice allows us to make decisions about new instructional practices and to design activities that align with what we know about effective teaching and learning. Chapter 3 contains an overview of the core principles and practices of writing centers, including collaboration and conversation as primary methods of teaching and learning in the writing center. Throughout this book, we focus on working with student-led writing centers because this method harnesses the social and instructional power of students working and learning together. In the process of teaching the tutoring lessons, teachers will also learn how to have better conversations about writing with students and colleagues. We are excited that you are joining us in exploring the power of elementary writing centers.

A NOTE ABOUT TERMINOLOGY

Throughout this book, we use various terms to describe what the students are doing: *peer conferencing, peer tutoring,* and *coaching.* We differentiate between peer conferencing and peer tutoring in the following way: *Peer conferencing* is a peer-to-peer conversation about one of the partner's writing; students are usually from within the same classroom or at least within the same grade level. Peer conferencing implies generally equal knowledge between the partners about writing. Peer tutoring typically involves students from different classrooms and possibly from different grade levels as well. In a peer tutoring setting, there is an assumption that the tutor will be the "more knowledgeable other" in the procedural knowledge of writing and revision (Harris, 1995; Vygotsky, 1978). The tutor has received specific training to develop the knowledge and skills necessary to support a peer writer. However, writing center tutoring is not as directive as more traditional tutoring structures; neither is it a one-way learning experience. We will discuss this more in Chapter 3.

We use the term coach as synonymous with peer tutor. This term came to us from the elementary students with whom we worked. They liked the idea of the positive, supportive nature of a coach—a cheerleader, so to speak—and it was a concept with which they were familiar. The coach helps the learner by giving small tips on how to meet the goals, by practicing alongside the learner, by helping him or her make effective choices in the moment, and by saying, "You can do this!" We use *coach* and *tutor* interchangeably throughout.

CHAPTER 2

Building a Strong Foundation with Writing Process Theory

with Sheri Vasinda

Teaching with a writing process approach has the power to build the confidence and competence of a young writer. When we give children time to write, on a daily basis, and show them what they are doing well, they begin to believe their way into writing. Writing process pedagogy has the potential to be student-centered, individualized instruction at its best. Each student writes at his or her own pace and level, and we teach them from where they are. Teaching with a process approach to writing also helps us explore the intricate connections between a student's purpose(s) for a piece of writing, his or her knowledge of the topic, and the thinking and composing processes involved in creating the product. There is much room for discovery, surprise, and growth. For all these reasons, and many more, we believe in the power of a writing process classroom.

Teachers with a strong theoretical understanding of writing (and teaching and learning, in general) are able to shape curricula to match those foundational beliefs no matter what the contextual constraints or circumstances might be. Even when faced with district mandates, pressure for high test scores and "accountability," and a jam-packed curriculum, theoretically grounded teachers will find a way to stay true to their beliefs about good writing instruction. When we know what is essential to good writing instruction, we can reflect on the teaching and learning in our classrooms, particularly when they *don't* work, and find ways to modify the practices without giving up on the essentials of good writing instruction. This chapter provides basic theoretical and practical information upon which a strong writing curriculum can be built. We have included an overview of 12 key principles in writing process theory and pedagogy. These theories and practices form the foundation of a typical process pedagogy and shape the instructional decisions we make as writing teachers.

TENETS OF WRITING PROCESS THEORY AND PEDAGOGY

It is not easy to teach writing and teach it well. There are reasons why so many teachers don't teach writing at all and would rather avoid it like the plague. "One of the factors that makes writing so difficult, as we know, is that we have *no recipes*" (Ede & Lundsford, 1984, p. 87, emphasis added). While there are no recipes for "good writing"—or good writing instruction—the rich body of research we have on composition and on children's writing processes points toward some essential structures for writing and effective writing pedagogy. Writing is a form of art—a process of creation—that needs suitable conditions for inspiration, germination, and development. It is not a paint-by-numbers activity; there are no rigid lines within which writers must stay, no step-by-step directions. However, supportive structures and conditions, such as time to study the works of others, guidance in selecting a subject matter or topic, time and strategies for revision, opportunities to share one's writing with others, and belief in one's creative abilities are necessary for development. These and other tenets of writing process theory and pedagogy are highlighted in the list below, and each of these will be elaborated upon in the discussions that follow. Of course, how these tenets are enacted will look different in each teacher's classroom. Inevitably, it was difficult to narrow down the most important ideas in writing instruction and we had to forgo discussion of components that we hope you will explore when you are ready for deeper investigation into topics such as voice, genre as both constraint and choice, the role of multimodality (image, drawing, music) in writing, and so forth. The tenets included here are ones we consider foundational.

- "Everyone can write" (Elbow, 2000).
- The writing process is inherently social and requires authentic audiences and purposes.
- Reading and writing are reciprocal processes that nurture each other.
- There are common—yet flexible—composing processes involved in writing.

- Topic knowledge and choice are essential for developing rich writing and writers.
- Writers need to be apprenticed into writing.
- Drafting is a process of discovery, meaning-making, and inquiry for the writer.
- Revision is the core of the writing process.
- Writers of all ages need time to write daily in an extended manner.
- There is great variation in the quality of a writer's work, and growth is spurred by the opportunity to solve problems in one's writing.
- Grammar and conventions are best taught within the context of meaningful, authentic texts.
- Writing is socially and culturally influenced.

"Everyone can write." A central belief of writing process educators is that "everyone can write" (Elbow, 2000). Even the drawings (Gardner, 1980), symbol producing (Dyson, 1993), and mock-letter writing (Calkins, 1994) of very young children are meaning-making processes and are emergent forms of writing that should be nurtured and developed (Graves, 2003). Writing process theory and practice is, at its very core, a competency-based pedagogy. Writing process teachers begin from where students are, examine what they do well, and highlight and celebrate those strengths with the writer. Each writer will be at a different stage in his or her writing development, and writers are in a perpetual process of growth. One is never "done" growing and learning as a writer. Therefore, the writing teacher's job is to closely analyze what a writer *can* do, instead of focusing on what he or she *can't* do, and begin the instructional conversation by celebrating the student's strengths and then moving toward the need (Calkins, 1994; Graves, 2003; Routman, 2005).

In deciding what to teach next, teachers look for writing elements that are "beginning to show but need to grow" in the student's writing (this is a phrase Jenn and a colleague, Suzii Parsons, developed in their work with teachers). For example, if a student writes an informational piece about wolves and puts information about what the wolf eats in three different places in the text, he may be ready to learn how to create and organize paragraphs and sections that focus on one idea until completion. Or, if a student writes a story about playing at the park with her cousins but glosses over the central event of playing at the park, she may be ready to learn how to stretch out an action moment in a story with imagery and concrete details. The writing teacher's job is to work with writers from wherever they are, and help them develop the confidence, skills, and strategies to become stronger writers.

The writing process is inherently social and requires authentic audiences and purposes. People write to communicate with others, and therefore, writing is an inherently social act that requires authentic audiences and purposes. Chapman (2006) states, "Children benefit from engaging in authentic writing tasks that involve them in the immediate uses of writing for enjoyment and communication, rather than as skills to be learned for some unspecified future use" (p. 34). Let's face it: Some pieces of writing are more meaningful than others. Some pieces of writing have real audiences and have potential to make an impact outside the walls of our classrooms. With the advent of Internet tools, such as blogs, video-upload sites, wikis, and social media platforms, authentic audiences are easily within the reach of young writers (Duke, 2013; Harvey, Goudvis, Muhtaris, & Ziemke, 2013; Warlick, 2009). But many writing assignments are given solely for the purposes of "doing school." Writing assignments serve a variety of curricular purposes, but it is important that at least some (if not the majority) of the students' writing is shared beyond the walls of the classroom so that students come to know the power and purposes of writing (Bomer & Bomer, 2001; Duke, Caughlin, Juzwik, & Martin, 2011).

Most writing is meant to be read by others, but even writing that is intended to remain private is, at least, a conversation with one's self. When a student writes, he or she may be addressing the self, the teacher, a wider known audience, or an unknown audience (Britton, Burgess, & Martin, 1975). Ede and Lunsford (1984) include friends, colleagues, critics, past and future audiences, and anomalous audiences in their list of possible addressees for a writer. In addition, classmates might serve as an authentic audience for students.

The influences of reader on writer and writer on reader are what make writing an inherently social process. The audience—real or imagined—along with the author's purpose shape the genre of the piece and the type of language used to convey his or her message (DeVitt, 2008). For example, when someone writes a letter, the structure of that letter and the language used will be influenced by the intended recipient. If the letter is for a friend, it will likely have a very different tone, form, and content from those of a business letter. Since audience plays such a significant role in the development of a piece, we need to help students find authentic audiences for their writing.

Reading and writing are reciprocal processes that nurture each other. Writing develops one's reading abilities, and reading develops one's writing abilities. Students benefit from learning to read like a writer and learning to write like a reader (Graham & Hebert, 2011). When students read like a writer, they are reading to discover the writer's strategies, style, use of literary devices, and organizational patterns. A student might notice how Mo Willems tells most of his stories entirely through dialogue, and he or she might want to try that writing style out in his or her own story. Another student might imitate Sy Montgomery's use of metaphor in informational writing. When students read through the lens of a writer, they are apprenticing themselves to that author and text, a process shown to be effective in the research (Graham & Perin, 2007). Likewise, a student can write like a reader—considering what the reader would think, what the reader would want to know, or how the reader might react to a certain event or piece of information. Considering the audience is a complex and crucial part of the writing process (Ede & Lunsford, 1984). When students write like a reader, they also consider the expectations for a genre—the norms that a reader would expect from a fantasy story, an informational text, a poem, and so on. Writing with the reader in mind helps the writer strengthen his or her understanding of genre characteristics.

Shanahan and Lomax (1986) examined the reading and writing products of 256 2nd- and 5th-graders and concluded, "Reading influences writing, and writing influences reading; theories of literacy development need to emphasize both of these characteristics similarly" (p. 208). They argued for an interactive model of the relationship between reading and writing performance and suggested that "reading and writing should be taught in ways that maximize the possibility of using information drawn from both reading and writing" (p. 208).

In sum, "reading and writing share common language routines and reasoning strategies," but they "involve quite different patterns of cognitive behaviors and different approaches to meaning-making" (Langer, 1986, p. 25). Both processes need to be taught explicitly, and they are taught most effectively when students engage in reading and writing as reciprocal and integrated processes.

There are common—yet flexible—composing processes involved in writing. Traditionally, the writing process has been simplified into a five-step process of writing development: (1) prewriting that may include brainstorming, generating ideas, rehearsal in a writer's notebook, or planning; (2) drafting or composing; (3) revising; 4) editing; and 5) publishing. However, some composition scholars have argued that this type of "stage model" of writing is artificial (Emig, 1971; Flower & Hayes, 1981). The old instructional method of brainstorming on Monday, drafting on Tuesday, revising on Wednesday, editing on Thursday, and publishing on Friday is an oversimplification and rigid application of the writing process and is not representative of what real writers do. Rather, the writing process is fluid, recursive, and individual. Just as all children do not develop in exactly the same sequence or manner, all writers do not go through exactly the same processes in exactly the same order.

Donald Graves, often considered the father of writing process pedagogy, spent two years (with Lucy Calkins and Susan Sowers) in a school observing, identifying, describing, and sequencing 16 children's composing processes during their primary school years (children ages 6 to 9). This research (Graves, 1982) was instrumental in identifying the processes of children's writing, namely, topic selection, rehearsal or preparation for writing, accessing information, spelling, handwriting, composing, reading, organizing, revising, and editing. While these processes are certainly not comprehensive, and it is not necessary to memorize them, this list gave educators insight into the activities involved in children's composing. One of the most important findings of Graves' research is that the writing process is idiosyncratic, meaning that it is unique for each individual and may be different each time a writer crafts a new piece.

George Hillocks Jr. (1987) reviewed approximately 2,000 studies of composition and the writing process and concluded that the "processes and sub-processes of composing are hierarchically related and recursive" (p. 71). Although each subprocess builds upon the previous one, the writing process is not a linear, lockstep sequence of activities. The writing process involves an organic interaction of several major elements: the writing environment, which includes the demands of the particular writing task (Flower & Hayes, 1981;

Hayes, 2012); the social context; social expectations for the genre (DeVitt, 2008); the writer's background knowledge of the topic; considerations of audience (Ede & Lunsford, 1984); and the cognitive processes of planning, putting words on paper (transcribing), reviewing, evaluating, and revising one's work (Flower & Hayes, 1981; Hayes, 2012). Writers may move flexibly back and forth between these elements and processes, which interact with each other in generative ways that influence the development and meaning-meaning that takes place. Understanding that the writing process is idiosyncratic, flexible, and recursive has great importance in how we design our writing curricula.

Topic knowledge and choice are essential for developing rich writing and writers. Research supports the idea that children's writing tends to be better when based on their own experiences (Braddock, Lloyd-Jones, & Schoer, 1963; Graves, 1982; Graves, 2003). Writers develop ideas and create meaning "out of the raw material of experience" (Flower & Hayes, 1980, p. 468). It is that wellspring of personal experience that fuels a writer's ideas and expression (Perl & Egendorf, 1979). Macrorie, an influential composition scholar, asserts that good writing requires truth and honesty rather than the artificial voice and superficial content that often comes with writing-for-the-teacher writing (Macrorie, 1985). This honesty comes from the writer's personal experiences. Honest, engaging writing cannot be achieved when a writer knows nothing about his or her topic or has no personal experiences from which to draw. (Of course, knowledge and experience can also be constructed through dialogue, reading, and other interactions with the social or natural worlds.)

Topic knowledge greatly influences the quality of the writing in both informational and narrative texts (Graves, 1982; Scardamalia, Bereiter, & Woodruff, 1980). The more a writer knows about his or her topic, the more detailed and rich the piece can be. This makes sense. Think about having to write on a topic you know very little about, say, Mopar muscle cars, for example. Unless you're a Mopar enthusiast, you may struggle to get even a single sentence written. Therefore, Graves (2003) recommends that students write about what they know and be given choice at least 70% of the time during writing/language arts instruction. Even within required genres or units of study, there is still significant room for students to select topics that resonate with them.

When students write on topics of their choice, teachers need ways to help them collect and develop personally meaningful ideas. Research (Hillocks, 1987) has shown that students need strategies for collecting and transforming information. Freewrites (Elbow, 2000), quickwrites (Graves & Kittle, 2005), and writer's notebooks (Fletcher, 1996) are very useful tools in this process. *Freewriting* is a process in which students write for a certain length of time, often 5 to 10 minutes (depending on the age of the writers and purpose of the freewrite), either on a broad topic suggested by the teacher or on any topic they wish to write about (Elbow, 2000). The goal of freewriting is to write the entire time without any long pauses. Students can even write, "I don't know what to write. I don't know what to write. I don't know what to write," . . . until they do; most of the time, an idea will come once the pen starts moving.

Quickwrites are often based on a given topic or piece of children's literature but remain open-ended (Graves & Kittle, 2005). The difference between a quickwrite or freewrite and a traditional writing prompt is that they leave lots of room for writers to make personal connections. For example, a quickwrite could begin with reading aloud a simple children's book called *Don't Worry Bear* (Foley, 2008), and after the read-aloud, asking students to write about an important friendship in their lives or a time they were really worried about someone. A quickwrite on either of these two central themes in the book allows students a lot of latitude in interpretation and room to make personal connections. A quickwrite should draw out students' personal stories rather than forcing them to conform to a narrow prompt such as "write about your favorite part of the state fair" (an actual prompt recently assigned to a middle school

---

RESOURCES FOR GETTING WRITERS STARTED

Buckner, Aimee. (2005). *Notebook Know-How: Strategies for the Writer's Notebook.* Portland, ME: Stenhouse.
Fletcher, Ralph. (1996). *A Writer's Notebook.* New York, NY: Harper Trophy
Graves, Donald, & Kittle, Penny. (2005). *My Quick Writes.* Portsmouth, NH: Heinemann.
Lane, Barry. (1993). *After the End.* Portsmouth, NH: Heinemann.

class). See the sidebar titled "Resources for Getting Writers Started" for some of our favorite teacher resources on writer's notebooks and quickwrites.

We know some of you are thinking, "But students have to write to a prompt on a test, so giving them topic choice won't prepare them for the test." Oh, but it does! Research has shown that students who learn in writing process classrooms—with choice, authentic purposes and audiences, and lots of time to write regularly—show positive growth in their writing performance (Dean-Rumsey, 1998; Pritchard & Honeycutt, 2006; Robinson, 1986) and perform as well as or better than those who learn to write from prompts and isolated writing activities and drills (Goldstein & Carr, 1996; Shelton & Fu, 2004). We should teach test-writing as a genre, as a discrete type of writing for a specific time and purpose, but this type of writing should not consume the curriculum. The majority of our writing instruction should involve authentic writing engagements with student choice and real audiences.

Writers need to be apprenticed into writing. Just as fledgling painters of the Renaissance imitated the techniques of the masters before developing their own style, students need to be apprenticed into the language arts. They need carefully selected writing models (also called *mentor texts*), explicit instruction on identifying writers' techniques and strategies, and help identifying exemplary writing traits or genre characteristics. In addition, students need guidance in producing specific types of writing (Calkins, 1994; Graham & Perin, 2007; Graves, 2003; Harvey, 1998; Hillocks, 1987; Lancia, 1997). Writing models can be professional and published (for example, high-quality children's literature or journalism) or novice and familiar (such as teachers' or students' own writing).

In addition to having examples of high-quality writing, students need teachers to help them notice and name the strategies used to make that writing engaging and effective. These strategies are often referred to as the "craft" of writing (Fletcher & Portalupi, 2007; Hale, 2008; Portalupi & Fletcher, 2001; Wood Ray, 1999). Several writing educators have identified specific writing craft elements (such as strong leads, repetition, or identifying an object with a specific brand name,) that make writing powerful, and these can and should be explicitly taught (Fletcher & Portalupi, 2007; Hale, 2008; Portalupi & Fletcher, 2001).

By modeling what proficient writers do, we are apprenticing children into the language and strategies of writers and the possibilities of different genres. Vygotsky (1978) states that children are apprenticed into language by more knowledgeable others, and Tardy and Swales (2008) call this process "cognitive apprenticeship" (p. 572). As with learning in any art medium, writers need the opportunity to be apprenticed into writing by studying work of other writers and imitating a writer's craft while developing their own style and skill set.

Drafting is a process of discovery, meaning-making, and inquiry for the writer. Through the act of writing, writers discover what they know about a subject, explore their purposes and goals for a piece of writing, and engage in the questioning processes of inquiry (Emig, 1971; Murray, 1978b, 1980; Zamel, 1982). The writer's job is "to develop new meanings" by bringing his or her unique perspectives and insights to bear on experiences in the world (Hillocks, 1995, p. xvii).

Writers often discover what they want to say while writing (Britton, Burgess, Martin, McLeod, & Rosen, 2009; Emig, 1971; Zamel, 1982). Peter Elbow (1973) says that people write their way into knowing:

> Think of writing as an organic, developmental process in which you start writing at the very beginning—before you know your meaning at all—and encourage your words gradually to change and evolve. Only at the end will you know what you want to say or the words you want to say it with. (p. 15)

In addition, a writer might develop new ideas and relationships between ideas during the process of writing (Hillocks, 1995). Writers grow meaning and significance into and out of their writing while they draft (Berlin, 2003; Calkins, 1994), indicating that discovery is at the core of the writing process (Murray, 1978a; Murray, 1980).

While writing involves discovery, it is also quite dependent upon inquiry (Hillocks, 1995). Two types of inquiry are at work in the writing process: wondering inquiries and information-seeking inquiries (Lindfors, 1999). Wondering inquiries are questions only the writer can answer, such as "What is the significance of this moment, this idea, or this information that I am writing about?" or "How does this thing relate to other things in my life or in the world?" These processes of wondering are central to the writing process. Writers also engage in information-seeking inquiry (that is, research). This research may come from firsthand observations of the world, wide reading, or other forms of information gathering (Fletcher, 1996; Hillocks, 1995). Research can be equally as important in fiction writing as in nonfiction. Students need instruction on how to gather, sort, integrate, and synthesize their research information into their own creations.

A teacher's own writing serves as an excellent resource for demonstrating the real stages of thinking—the drafting processes—that a writer might go through (Graves, 2003; Zumbrunn & Krause, 2012). Many teachers are familiar with the *think-aloud* strategy for modeling a reader's internal, mental comprehension processes (Wilhelm, 2001). Think-alouds on the writing process are just as necessary in helping students understand the internal, mental composing processes of writers (Englert et al., 1991; Englert, Raphael, & Anderson, 1992). Students need to see the starts, stops, restarts, cross-outs, and multiple versions of a writer's work and hear a writer talk through these decisions on his or her way to meaning-making. They need to see authentic draft writing—in all its messy splendor—and they need the freedom of time and space to draft. Since discovery and meaning-making happen during the drafting process, teachers should not expect students to begin a piece of writing with a complete map or outline of the text and be bound rigidly to that plan. There must be room for a writer to develop knowledge, insight, intention, and connections along the way.

Revision is the core of the writing process. People rarely produce a finished piece of writing, ready to "publish," in one draft; it is more likely that a quality piece requires multiple revisions. Lucy Calkins (1994) describes revision (or "re-vision") as a time to "re-see," to look again at a piece of writing and imagine its possibilities. Donald Murray (1978a) defines revision similarly as "the process of seeing what you've said to discover what you have to say" (p. 56). Revision involves considering the best form or structure for a piece, whether or not the writing meets the writer's intentions, how it captures and maintains the reader's attention, message clarity, topic focus, and much more. Revision is essential in the process of growing meaning in a piece and matching intention to product.

Lucy Calkins' (1983) research documented the developmental revision processes of primary grades children: First, a child might engage in random drafting in which he or she doesn't look back at previous drafts. The young writer's second draft may be completely different from the first or may look more like editing (limited to minor refinements in spelling, penmanship, or phrasing) than true revision. These are normal phases of development for beginning writers. As writers progress in their ability to revise, they enter the "transition stage" in which they can look back at previous drafts, reread, and make more substantial changes. A more competent reviser can move successfully between multiple drafts and consider his or her needs as a writer, the audience, and subject matter. Calkins' stages are applicable to novice writers of any age.

During the revision processes, a writer engages in problem solving: problems of focus, locating and selecting relevant information, space limitations, audience, purpose, voice, and so forth. These problem-solving acts are at the heart of revision and spur the growth of a writer: "You don't learn to write by going through a series of preset writing exercises. You learn to write by grappling with a real subject that truly matters to you" and by grappling with real writing challenges (Fletcher, 1993, p. 4). Therefore, writers need to be taught a handful of effective revision (or problem-solving) strategies that they can apply flexibly to various genres and pieces. In addition, children revise more effectively when they have clear criteria for revision (Hillocks, 1987), perhaps in the form of a checklist or rubric created with the teacher. However, we should be careful that students don't become too reliant upon such rubrics or checklists. The focus of revision should be on matching the text to the writer's intentions and making it the strongest it can be for the time being.

A word of caution with revision: Not every piece of writing needs to be revised, edited, or published. It is not practical or reflective of real writing processes to revise and publish every piece of writing a writer starts. James Dickey, a noted American poet, once said, "I have endless drafts, one after another. . . . I work on the process of refining low-grade ore. I get maybe a couple of nuggets of gold out of 50 tons of dirt" (Perl & Schwartz, 2006, p. 20). Most writers have notebooks full of entries and pieces that remain in draft form. We write to contemplate and grow ideas and to explore our thoughts. Writing regularly gives us sufficient opportunity to experiment with style, technique, literary devices, and genres—to build our repertoire. But most of that writing will never be shared publicly; nor should it be (for further discussion of low-stakes and private writing, see Elbow, 2000). Practically speaking, elementary and middle school students might publish two or three pieces each grading quarter.

Writers of all ages need time to write daily in an extended manner. Writing takes time; there is no way around it. In order to engage the types of discovery and inquiry mentioned above, students need to write daily, for extended periods of time, from kindergarten up (Calkins, 1994; Elbow, 2000; Graves, 2003). The Common Core State Standards for English Language Arts and Literacy stress the importance of regular writing time for students to develop as writers; Anchor Standard 10 states that children should "write routinely over extended time frames (time for research, reflection, and revision) and shorter time frames (a single sitting or day or two) for a range of discipline-specific tasks, purposes, and audiences" (National Governors Association Center for Best Practices & Council of Chief State School Officers, 2010, p. 21).

Just as primary grade teachers help young readers build reading stamina incrementally, writing teachers have to help build a writer's stamina incrementally and developmentally. Emerging writers may begin by drawing and labeling compositions, working initially for short periods of time, gradually increasing their work time and moving toward compositions that include more text. In 1st grade, a teacher might start with 10- or 15-minute writing sessions at the beginning of the year and work up to 30-minute writing sessions (or longer!).

Donald Graves (2003) says that if you're going to give students time to write only 1 or 2 days a week, don't bother. With such limited time, students can't gain any momentum in their writing and don't have sufficient time to develop their skills. Imagine if a pianist practiced only once or twice a week; rarely would he or she ever fully learn a piece, and it would be difficult to gain any proficiency. The same goes for writing: Writers need time to develop their skills. They need to write 4 to 5 days a week on meaningful topics that allow for multifaceted composing processes.

There is great variation in the quality of a writer's work, and growth is spurred by the opportunity to solve problems in one's writing. Research reveals that the quality of an individual's writing varies from day to day and piece to piece (Anderson, 2005; Graves, 2003; Karalitz, 1988; Kincaid, 1952). Variation is to be expected, and teachers shouldn't be alarmed when the quality of a student's work takes a temporary dip as he or she explores new genres and techniques (Graves, 2003). We can promote a general upward growth trajectory by allowing writers the time and space to experiment and encounter tensions between what they wanted to accomplish with the piece (the writer's intentions) and the actual product in front of them (the actualization) as well as supporting them in problem solving to resolve those tensions. Graves says, "Losing balance, regaining it, and going on is the substance of learning" (2003, p. 231).

Research also shows that, because a writer's performance varies so greatly over time, "a single paper written by a student on a given topic at a particular time cannot be considered as a valid basis for evaluating [a student's] achievement" (Kincaid, 1952, p. 93). This means teachers need to look at student writing over time, gather many samples of a student's writing, and examine the patterns of writing behaviors and strategies employed by the writer in order to accurately assess his or her abilities and decide what skills to teach next (Calfee & Miller, 2013). A single, timed writing prompt cannot accurately represent the variation in a student's writing. Instead, examining a writer's performance with multiple writing samples across a number of genres provides a more well-rounded assessment of a child's writing abilities. To accurately and authentically assess a writer's proficiency, he or she needs to be evaluated both formatively and summatively on a collection of work over time (Calfee & Miller, 2013)—rather than by a single, "on-demand" standardized assessment.

Grammar and conventions are best taught within the context of meaningful, authentic texts. Study after study has shown that grammar is best learned in the context of students' own writing or other authentic writing rather than through isolated drill-and-practice grammar instruction (Calkins, 1980; Harris, 1962; Hillocks, 1987). Calkins (1980) found that 1st-grade students who learned grammar in context knew how to describe or use more than twice the number (nine vs. four) of punctuation elements than students taught with the traditional, isolated skill method. Studies repeatedly confirm that "instruction in formal grammar has little or no effect on the quality of student composition" (Braddock et al., 1963, p. 37). Teachers know this. Isolated grammar instruction such as "Daily Oral Language" (Byers, 2001) or correct-all worksheets doesn't transfer to actual improvements in students writing. Furthermore, research has shown that isolated grammar instruction has a *harmful* effect on students' writing when it displaces or replaces rich writing instruction (Anderson, 2005; Braddock et al., 1963; National Council of Teachers of English, 1985).

However, explicit instruction in grammar is needed, but it is more powerful when it is linked to authentic writing models, examples, and the students' own writing. Self-editing is one effective way for students to learn to reduce the number of grammatical and mechanical errors in their papers (Lyman, 1931). Another way to teach grammar effectively is to use model texts, or mentor sentences, to showcase how grammar and mechanics influence the meaning of a sentence or passage and have students imitate these grammatical structures to shape their writing (Anderson, 2005; Weaver, 1996). Additionally, grammar instruction through teacher–student editing conferences when a piece is ready to be published is a powerful, personalized, and point-of-need instructional strategy. During editing conferences, select one or two skills to teach that the child is "using but confusing," indicating he or she is ready to learn how to properly apply that device (Bear, Invernizzi, Templeton, & Johnston, 2013). Choose just *one or two* skills to teach in the context of a particular piece of writing, showing the child how the convention changes the meaning of the text. The purpose for selecting just one or two skills to teach is so that the child can fully grasp those skills and apply them to not only this piece but also transfer them to future writings. Don't worry about the other errors at this time; these errors will arise again in other pieces and can be addressed when they are most pressing.

Our goal as writing teachers should be for students to learn to use conventions intentionally—as meaning-making tools—to craft and clarify their own writing. Child writing is cherished because it is just that, child writing, filled with all its invented spellings, child language, and grammatical blunders. Therefore, the degree of editing done with a piece should be dictated by the age and stage of the writer as well as the purpose and audience for the writing.

Writing is socially and culturally influenced. A strong writing curriculum acknowledges and builds upon children's existing social and cultural uses for language and literacy. From rich ethnographic studies (e.g., Heath, 1983; Lopez, 1999), educators have learned that people of different cultures use writing in their home and community for different purposes: for entertainment, for religious learning and practice, to plan social events, or to conduct the business of running a home. Teachers can draw upon these home literacies to engage and motivate students in writing practices that have personal relevance. Students can share their "funds of knowledge"—the linguistic and literacy skills they practice at home as well as their cultural values and knowledge—and use these as starting points for making connections to other genres and texts (Moll, Amanti, Neff, & Gonzalez, 1992).

Ann Haas Dyson (1993) highlighted the ways social and popular culture information gets appropriated by young writers and used to compose their texts. Teachers of primary grade children will recall students often using their friends' names in writing to establish and maintain social relationships. Young writers also transform popular songs, cartoon characters, and familiar stories in their own writing. Rather than viewing students' use of superheroes and popular book or media characters as "copying" or "uncreative," Dyson encourages us to notice how students transform these popular culture icons into their own unique plots and settings. All writers take inspiration from the texts they love; for many young children today, those texts are based in a variety of media rather than in classical literature.

Dyson's work has also helped writing teachers understand the importance of conversation in the writing classroom, particularly for primary grade writers but also for older writers. Writing, for many children, is a social *process* and not just a social product. Students need opportunities to bounce their ideas off of a classmate during the composing process or brainstorm out loud with a friend. For these children, the silent classroom can cripple their writing process.

Difficulties may also arise when the school's practices are very different from children's home cultures or when teachers don't recognize and value the types of literacy children bring from home (Duke & Purcell-Gates, 2003). Scollon and Scollon (1981) wrote about Athabaskan Native Americans who had particular cultural ways of sharing knowledge and telling stories that were in opposition to the school's expectations for writing. When asked to write a traditional school essay, the students had a very difficult time conforming to academic essay standards partly because the essay format contradicted their cultural ways of communicating and sharing knowledge. Similarly, James Gee (1996) tells a story about Leona, a girl whose African American storytelling patterns were not aligned with her Caucasian teacher's expectations for efficient storytelling during a class share time. Therefore, Leona's story was hurried along and not valued in the same ways that other classmates' stories were. Writing is socially and culturally influenced, and we need to be conscious of children's social and cultural worlds and the ways in which their experiences with language and their cultural values shape their writing (Dyson, 1993; Fu, 1995; Gee, 1996; Lopez, 1999).

CONCLUSION

Teaching writing is challenging and complex. But it is also hugely rewarding. You get to learn about your students and their lives through writing in ways that are not possible in teaching other subjects, and you teach them skills that will carry them through their lives and their academic or professional careers. Although the components of a writing process classroom may seem like a lot to negotiate for a teacher who is new to writing process instruction, beginning writing teachers can start with a simple structure of daily writing on topics students choose with a couple of focused lessons each week (see Chapter 6) on key writing elements. And grow from there.

As you move through the ideas in the rest of this book, keep this strong foundation of writing process theory in mind. In developing writing assignments and engagements, teaching students about the elements of good writing, training the writing tutors, and guiding tutors in their writing center sessions, keep this core writing process theory at the forefront of your decisions and pedagogy.

CHAPTER 3

Writing Center Principles and Pedagogy

Writing centers create spaces for powerful knowledge-making. When peers are reading and talking about writing together, the benefits of writing center engagements are great for teachers, tutors, and writers. In order to understand how this unique kind of knowledge-making works, we need to examine writing center principles and how those principles shape the interactions and pedagogy of the writing center. We begin with a brief overview of the evolution of writing centers and writing center pedagogy so that you understand the roots of writing centers and the history behind the practice. Then, we dig into the core operating principles of writing centers and introduce guidelines and strategies for tutors to use in leading the writing center sessions.

THE EVOLUTION OF WRITING CENTERS AND WRITING CENTER PEDAGOGY

Writing centers have a long history in the United States. During the late 19th and early 20th centuries, writing centers were envisioned as writing laboratories, spaces where students would work during class time to polish their writing (Lerner, 2009). Early writing laboratories were "conceived of not as a *place* but rather as a *method* of instruction" (Boquet, 1999, p. 466). In this environment, rather than through lectures, students were actually writing during class time and self-correcting or having the instructors correct their errors. In the 1940s, writing labs started the move to autonomous spaces as freestanding locations but were still closely tied to the classroom. This trend continued into the 1950s with the writing labs becoming more of an institutional resource than simply English course labs. Writing centers seemed to disappear in the late 1950s through the 1960s with the rise of linguistics as a field, a shift that mirrored the scientific advances of the Cold War (Carino, 1995).

Many current writing centers trace their origins back to the 1970s when writing centers began to proliferate as a means of addressing student writing concerns that arose with university open admissions policies. Such policies increased enrollments and included a more diverse student population along with a perception that these students' literacy skills were less than ideal. Writing centers at that time were perceived as a means to "remediate" a student population unprepared for university-level writing. The number of writing centers in North America and the world has increased dramatically since that era. With the increase in sites and needs, writing center philosophy and pedagogy has grown and changed.

Writing center studies as a field of scholarship took center stage with Stephen North's 1984 article, "The Idea of a Writing Center." In this article, North resists stereotypes of the writing center as a "fix it" shop, a space in which a writer can get grammar problems solved or a place where remediation is the dominant stance. His exhortation is that "in a writing center the object is to make sure that writers, and not necessarily their texts, are what are changed by instruction. In axiom form, it goes like this: our job is to make better writers not better writing. . . . In the center, though, we look through or beyond that particular project, that particular text, and see it as an occasion for addressing *our* primary concern, the process by which it is produced" (North, 1984, p. 438). The focus, then, is on the writer and on the writing process. This writing center principle is still very much a part of writing center conversations and practices today.

CORE WRITING CENTER PRINCIPLES

According to the International Writing Center Association, "Both tutor and tutee are inherently guided by essential 21st Century skills of critical thinking, creativity, collaboration, and communication" in the tutoring conference (IWCA, 2015). These 21st-century skills are ones that all teachers strive to foster through their curricula. Writing centers are uniquely positioned to nurture these skills and do so by enacting a set of core principles:

- Collaborative learning and conversation are the primary methods of teaching and learning in the writing center.
  - » "The one-to-one conversations about writing increase student learning, build a culture of student leadership, and reinforce writing instruction" (IWCA, 2015).
  - » Open-ended questioning strategies are an essential teaching/learning approach employed during the writing center sessions and serve to maintain a writer's autonomy and ownership of the writing.
- Writing tutors work to "make better writers" by sharing new writing strategies, processes, and genre knowledge (North, 1984, p. 438). They move the writing forward by helping writers talk through their thinking, their writing processes, and their challenges as well as engage writers in problem finding and problem solving. The focus of the writing center session is to move beyond the immediate text at hand to understand and deepen the writer's process.
- Writing centers train tutors to address revision of more global elements such as ideas and organization in student writing before local concerns of editing or proofreading (IWCA, 2015).
- Although the writing tutor is the one who is trained to lead the writing conversation, the writer is the one who holds the most power. The writer retains control of the writing. The writer is the one who identifies needs, concerns, and conversation topics. And the writer is the one who ultimately decides on any revisions or changes that are made to the writing.
- The writing center is a supportive, encouraging, positive space in which tutors work to improve the confidence and competence of writers.

These few core principles, complemented by the writing process tenets we presented in Chapter 2, guide the interactions in and pedagogy of writing centers. In the sections that follow, we will unpack and elaborate on these principles to illustrate what they look like in action.

COLLABORATIVE LEARNING IN THE WRITING CENTER

Collaborative learning and conversation are at the heart of what students do in writing centers. In the context of peer tutoring, students can discover ways to become part of the learning conversation, both socially and intellectually, and they acquire the "conventions" of these conversations: Tutors learn ways to build rapport, encourage a writer's confidence, get a writer to talk about his or her topic, ask productive questions, and offer suggestions in a kind and useful manner. Writers learn to talk about their writing process, elaborate on ideas, put their thoughts into words, communicate assignment parameters, convey their questions and struggles, and listen to constructive suggestions for improving the work. With this type of back-and-forth give-and-take between tutor and writer, the peer tutoring session becomes a collaborative alternative to teacher-directed instruction and the traditional, teacher-centered classroom.

Collaborative learning has several demonstrated benefits for students; according to Lunsford (1991), it can . . .

- engage the whole student;
- encourage active learning;
- aid in problem finding as well as problem solving;
- aid in learning abstractions—how to connect concrete and abstract concepts;
- aid in assimilation and transfer of new information;
- foster interdisciplinary and critical thinking;
- foster deeper understanding of others;
- promote higher achievement than competitive or individualistic approaches; and
- promote individual and communal excellence, that is, working together encourages us to produce quality work (pp. 5–6).

Despite the advantages of collaborative learning, Lunsford cautions that creating a collaborative environment can be difficult. To successfully implement a collaborative learning model, teachers must create curricular structures that support collaboration, design instruction that fosters higher-order problem defining and solving, incorporate tasks that require shared thinking and collaborative work, and draw upon individual student expertise and voice. Teachers must also have clearly defined goals, reject traditional teacher–learner hierarchies, and select the various learning groups (Lunsford, 1991). In order for collaborative learning to work well, the teacher must establish a safe learning community, be highly organized, and persist when challenges arise. Too often, when collaborative learning presents challenges, teachers abandon the effort altogether rather than teaching or reteaching the skills, strategies, and procedures necessary for effective collaborations.

When we collaborate, we are engaging in creating "knowledge that is socially constructed" (Lunsford, 1991, p. 8). This type of collaboratively created knowledge may be difficult for students to accept and value, especially if they come from school experiences or cultural backgrounds that promote and value teacher-as-knowledge-giver. Collaborative learning models, therefore, challenge traditional power dynamics and teacher–learner hierarchies. They put students in positions of power and situate them as active knowledge creators. We have found that—when properly supported—students tend to rise up to assume the added responsibility that comes along with this power shift. Students need, and may even crave, such responsibility, as Annie Ortiz so poignantly described in the introduction to this book.

Muriel Harris, in *Writing in the Middle: Why Writers Need Writing Tutors*, describes this collaborative context and the value of tutoring: "It [tutoring] introduces into the educational setting a middle person, the tutor, who inhabits a world somewhere between student and teacher" (1995, p. 28). This puts the tutor in a unique position to work effectively with the student because tutors don't make assignments, create deadlines, or give grades. The relationship is one of helping. While independence is encouraged, the tutor can help with strategic or procedural kinds of knowledge that are important to the writing process: the how-to and the meta-knowledge needed to reflect on and achieve writing goals (Harris, 1995; Hillocks, 1995). Tutors can also address the writer's affective concerns such as a lack of confidence in writing or writing anxieties. In addition, the tutor can help translate the teacher's expectations for the assignment or genre in a language that is more accessible for the student. The collaborative learning that results from peer tutoring helps the writer improve his or her abilities to produce an effective text and build strategies to use again in future writing tasks.

Practically speaking, collaboration is a necessary life skill for engaged members of society. Businesses and organizations want employees who are able to work with others to pose and solve problems, to innovate, to actively engage in the tasks at hand, to assume leadership roles, and to engage in interdisciplinary thinking. These are skills and attributes that are fostered through the collaborative learning that takes place in a writing center. Paula Gillespie, Brad Hughes, and

Harvey Kail (2007) have demonstrated that—in addition to benefits to the writers—there are benefits to the tutors themselves. Through their Peer Tutor Alumni Project, they discovered—from focus groups and surveys of students who were undergraduate peer tutors—that engaging in peer tutoring boosts confidence, gives tutors an advantage in job interviews, and provides "valuable training for the kinds of collaborative tasks common in the world of work" (p. 41). Their research results show that peer tutors are able to transfer their writing and communication skills to job interviews and career development. Although the focus of our own research (Chapter 5) was not specifically on benefits to tutors, our data also indicate that tutors may learn just as much as the writers.

PEER TUTORING VERSUS PEER RESPONSE

You may be wondering how the kind of peer tutoring we are talking about differs from the kind of peer response you might have students do in class. While the kind of collaborative learning that takes place in a writing center can also be achieved in the classroom, there are advantages to having peer tutors who engage with writers beyond their regular classroom. Peer tutoring contrasts with the traditional in-class peer response one might see in a writing workshop classroom:

- Often peer responses end up focusing on surface errors, particularly at the elementary school level (Fletcher, Portalupi, & Williams, 2006; Routman, 2005) or on feedback on the paper as a whole (Harris, 1992). In contrast, peer tutors help writers go beyond identifying conventions and grammatical errors. Rather, they move to questioning the writer and the text and helping the writer elaborate on the ideas in the piece.
- Peer responses are usually limited to one stage of the writing process or one point in time, typically the revision or editing stage (Calkins, 1994); whereas in peer tutoring, writers converse at any stage of the process—brainstorming, organization, verbal planning, drafting, revising, or editing—and potentially at more than one point.
- Peer tutors help with broader abilities: Rather than focusing on a particular aspect of the paper only, they look at that particular aspect of the paper with the broader subject in

mind. For example, the discussion about an introduction is not just about that particular introduction but how to write introductions in general (Harris, 1992).

- Tutors rely heavily on listening skills and the ability to ask questions (Harris, 1992; Meyer & Smith, 1987). Tutors work to figure out and realize the intentions of the writer, whereas peer response is often limited to aesthetic reader response ("I liked it") or feedback that focuses on the teacher's goals for the writing.
- The tutor is nonjudgmental and someone trusted as knowledgeable (Harris, 1992). Often peers in class are not considered skilled and students may feel the risk of sharing their writing with classmates is too great.
- The tutor helps the writer find his or her own questions and answers. Peer responses often revolve around informing and giving answers to the writer (Harris, 1992).

In sum, peer tutoring sessions help move the writing forward more than traditional peer response. These sessions also help the writer develop strategies that can assist him or her in future work. It's about helping the writer talk about the piece, work through the kinks, and notice the successes. It is a time for the writer to take center stage as the creator and reflect on how the piece is progressing, with the tutor serving as a facilitator for that conversation and growth.

WRITING CENTER PEDAGOGY

The instructional methods implemented during the tutoring sessions as well as the methods used by teachers to train the tutors are the basis of effective writing center interactions. Tutors often have to be cheerleader *and* coach to the writers. Much time is spent on creating a welcoming and friendly space for writing centers. Often writers come in feeling uncertain or anxious about their writing, and writing center tutors are prepared to play various roles in order to help the writer and the writing.

Writing center tutors assume that writing is a process and are aware of ways to help someone through the planning, writing, revising, and polishing stages of writing. If a writer is just beginning to plan the piece, a tutor may help with brainstorming by asking questions about an assignment, suggesting prewriting activities such as freewriting or concept mapping, or simply asking the writer to talk about the topic. If the writer has a draft, a tutor may need to decide whether the writing needs attention at the global level of content and organizational issues or attention at the local, sentence level with grammatical or stylistic issues that interfere with clarity. Toward the end of the process, a tutor may help a writer learn how to polish by attending to conventions, visual format, or other elements. Tutors are trained to be flexible and work with a writer at any point in the process.

Applying the writing center principles we introduced earlier, we developed the following general guidelines for tutors to structure their sessions:

- *Be sure to smile and introduce yourself.* Try to be friendly and keep the interactions as positive as possible. Learn about the writer throughout the session. Establishing a rapport can be challenging, but it's important for the writer to feel comfortable.

- *Establish the agenda for the session* by asking the writer about the assignment, his or her goals for the paper, and any concerns.

- *Don't write on the writer's paper.* The writer's agency is important; he or she needs to feel like he or she is in control of the ideas and the piece of writing and has ownership of any changes that are made to the piece.

- *Sit next to (rather than across from) the writer.* This is a collaborative position. It also physically allows the tutor and writer to read the paper at the same time.

- *Have the writer read the piece aloud.* It can be difficult to read someone else's handwriting, and having the writer read his or her own paper relieves this potential tension. It also helps the tutor and writer hear the rhythm and flow of the writing and notice rough spots and minor grammatical errors. (For secondary and postsecondary writers and tutors, it is a good idea to allow the writer to choose if he or she wants to read the piece or prefers the tutor to read it. At the elementary level, having the tutor read the writer's piece aloud often poses problems. Since elementary student writing relies heavily on invented spelling, it's too difficult for a peer to decipher.

The reader ends up stumbling heavily over the spelling and grammar errors, causing the writer to feel embarrassed and inadequate. Thus, we strongly recommend the routine of having the writer read his or her paper aloud.)

- **Be an active listener.** Validate the writer's concerns by "saying back" the ideas the writer expressed. The tutor might use language such as "It sounds like you are saying . . . ," paraphrasing what the writer has just said to check his or her understanding.
- **Ask about the writer's concerns.** Many times, the writer will be unhappy with a section of the writing or be stuck and unsure of how to proceed. Tutors can start by asking, "Is there any part of the writing you're struggling with?" They might also ask, "What is challenging about this piece of writing?"
- **Use open-ended rather than yes/no questions** to help the writer elaborate, clarify, and to give space for the writer to think out loud. (This is a big one! We teach students how to ask open-ended questions in tutor training lessons 2 and 3, in Chapter 6).
- **Give "wait time" to allow the reader to think.** This is a tough but effective tool available to tutors. Too often, teachers and tutors ask a question and then jump right in with a second question if the writer doesn't respond immediately. Writers may need time to think before answering a question the tutor has asked or time to work through a new idea introduced in the session. Tutors need to practice asking a question—and waiting—for the answer. If necessary, the writer may need some time to write, and the tutor can walk away from the table for a few minutes to give the writer space and time to think. Allowing silence sends the message that the writer needs to take responsibility for the thinking and writing.
- **Have resources nearby.** Keeping a dictionary, scrap paper, and the Question Charts (see the end of Chapter 6) will both allow easy access when needed and provide an opportunity for modeling the use of resources.
- **Focus on global-level components (content and organization) first,** and then look at the more local issues of sentence structure and conventions. If the ideas are unclear or the content is not focused, it is a waste of time to look at sentence or convention issues. For example, if a paragraph needs to be

deleted because it doesn't fit the topic, the time spent editing
the sentences in that paragraph will be wasted.

In addition to the general tutoring procedures listed above, Ryan
and Zimmerelli (2010) suggest that tutors use "I" language. Instead
of saying, "You did" this or that, the tutor would start the statement
with "I": "I noticed . . . ," "I wonder if . . . ," or "I'm a little confused
here . . ." They also recommend that tutors respond as a reader. People
write to be heard, to share their ideas and knowledge, to communicate
with others, and to express their emotions. Writers have an essential
need to share their work with others. (Of course, some writing re-
mains solely private.) Part of a tutor's job is to respond as an interested
and caring reader—to enjoy the piece on a personal, human level and
share that genuine reaction with the writer. Tutors can also express
their confusion, surprise, or need for additional information. By sharing these reader reactions, the tutor will likely help the writer clarify
confusing places, elaborate on details that were in the writer's head
but not on the paper, or show the writer places that worked really
well to elicit a particular emotion for the reader (Ryan & Zimmerelli,
2010). Responding as a reader may help the writer refocus if the writing wanders, or it may prompt the writer to expand on an idea. In
addition, asking the "so what" question, such as "What big idea do
you want your readers to take away from this piece?" or "Why is this
topic important to you?" helps writers focus on audience and purpose
as well as justify why information has been included.

These guidelines have been made into a student-friendly chart
called the WRITE mnemonic (located at the end of Chapter 6), which
you can photocopy for individual students and also use to create an
anchor chart (poster) for the writing center space. The guidelines need
to be explicitly taught to the tutors, and the lessons in Chapter 6 along
with the Question Charts for tutors (located at the end of Chapter 6)
will assist you in this process. The guidelines are simplified a bit in the
WRITE mnemonic, so the more detailed ideas listed above should be
shared verbally during the tutor training lessons.

CONCLUSION

The strategies and tutoring guidelines in this chapter form what is
commonly referred to as a writing center pedagogy. Writing centers

are often dubbed "friendly places" where one of the main goals is for writers to feel welcomed, supported, and encouraged. Tutors foster this atmosphere by allowing writers to maintain control and ownership of their pieces, listening carefully to the writer's concerns and challenges, responding in kind and interactive ways, and making suggestions for enriching the ideas in the piece. Of course, all this collaboration does not happen on its own. Students need instruction and guidance from a teacher during their tutoring sessions. Teachers can step in to facilitate a session when tutors are stuck, when they don't know how to move the conversation along productively, or when the teacher notices student interactions breaking down into unproductive ones. However, the lessons in Chapter 6 will help tutors learn to talk productively with others about writing.

When we were researching how to start a writing center in an elementary school, we found very few resources. Wilcox and Collins (2003) set up a writing center in which Brigham Young University education students acted as tutors to students at a local elementary school. However, their article suggested that children at the elementary level may not be the most effective tutors. As you will see in later chapters, this was not the case for our writing center. Our tutors were very effective! There is plenty of research on implementing writing centers at the secondary level, but these sources were less helpful to us in establishing elementary school writing centers because the elementary school contexts are quite different from even middle schools, much less high schools. So we headed into our project with confidence that peer tutoring would work because of our theoretical, philosophical, and instructional backgrounds, but we knew that it would need to be a collaborative endeavor with those most knowledgeable about their elementary school context—the classroom teachers.

CHAPTER 4

Establishing, Maintaining, and Sustaining the Writing Center

When Rebecca talks to faculty at the university about their writing center, she says it is a win-win-win situation: Student writers, student tutors, and instructors as well as the school all benefit from the peer tutoring interactions, as articulated by the International Writing Center Association's Position Statement on Secondary School Writing Centers (IWCA, 2015):

- Student writers benefit from writing centers in the following ways: through critical engagement with an invested partner to receive low-stakes feedback on and authentic responses to their writing; differentiated instruction; social interaction; increased confidence in and motivation for writing; and reinforcement of lifelong writing habits.
- Peer tutors benefit from writing centers through an increased understanding of the writing and collaborative learning process, improved oral and written communication skills, critical analysis, adaptability, leadership skills, and preparation for academic and professional communication.
- Teachers of all subject areas benefit from writing centers as they reflect on writing pedagogy, support formative assessment practices, and engage in professional dialogue with other teachers and with peer tutors and student writers.
- The school community benefits from writing centers as an institutional commitment to writing becomes public, [is] inclusive, and engages all stakeholders as students become true leaders among their peers in learning communities and as writers' voices are empowered (IWCA, 2015, writingcenters.org/about/iwca-position-statements).

Richard Kent (2010) describes how his high school writing center changed his teaching life. He no longer had to bring home stacks and stacks of papers to respond to and edit. He was no longer the sole audience for his students' writing, and thus students were much more motivated to engage in deep revision when their peers were reading and responding to their work. He was freed up to be a writing coach and had more time for richer writing conferences with students because he wasn't pressed to squeeze in time to check in with *every* student.

The potential benefits for students and teachers are equally as viable at the elementary level as the secondary level, and sharing these benefits with colleagues and other stakeholders may help start conversations about establishing a writing center at your school. When we want to bring about change or persuade others to try something new, especially in the context of the ever-pressed-for-time elementary school curriculum, we have to be able to clearly articulate how this approach enhances student learning. The benefits described by the IWCA shown above, the theory chapters in this book, and Chapter 5 on our own research data all serve to support you in this process of advocating for your writing center.

When we know where we are going and why we're on the journey in the first place, we can make effective decisions to get to our destination. This chapter provides an overview of some possible writing center models along with suggestions for establishing and maintaining a successful writing center in the elementary school setting. As much as every writing center shares some core principles and outcomes, every writing center is also unique because of its context. Therefore, we have included questions you will want to ask yourself or discuss with those involved in establishing your writing center in order to determine the best structure for your school.

THE WRITING CENTER DIRECTOR

As with any human endeavor, there must be a leader (or a team of leaders). Writing centers are no different. Someone needs to take the lead, to advocate for the center, and to organize its people; this is the writing center director. The director is the person who communicates the vision, plans, organizes, and provides the passion and cheerleading necessary to establish and maintain the writing center. He or she advocates for the center by highlighting the positive teaching and learning outcomes that are possible with this collaboration and by sharing the writing center's progress and successes with colleagues, administrators, parents, and even the larger community. The director shares information about writing center principles and pedagogy with others (Chapter 3) and leads conversations with colleagues about how those principles and practices might play out in your particular place. The director also gathers people together to plan and organize the writing center schedule, the tutor training lessons, and the comings and goings of the writing center. Should you find yourself in this exciting position, we wholeheartedly applaud you (applause, applause!) for being open to this work and enthusiastic about the possibilities for a writing center in your school.

BUILDING YOUR BACKGROUND KNOWLEDGE

In order to advocate for a particular pedagogical approach, teachers must be prepared with adequate background knowledge. If you haven't done so already, we encourage you to read Chapters 2 and 3 in this book about writing processes and the basics of writing center pedagogy, because these ideas will inform your thinking and curricular choices. In addition, the IWCA website (writingcenters.org/) is a treasure trove of information for establishing and maintaining writing centers, with resources for directors. A handful of K–12 writing center resource links are listed there as well (writingcenters.org/k-12-writing-center-links/). On the National Writing Project's website, under "Resource Topics," then "Teaching Writing," you will find a "Writing Centers" section with resources, including two NWP Radio talks that Rebecca and Jenn did discussing our first elementary writing center (www.nwp.org/cs/public/print/resource_topic/writing_centers). Rich Kent (2010) and Dawn Fels and Jennifer Wells (2011) also provide valuable insights into middle and high school writing centers in their books that may help you think about your elementary writing center.

DEVELOPING AN INSTRUCTIONAL FRAMEWORK

Planning for a writing center at your school will take time, and one important action is to build a foundation of support for the writing center. As you discuss the possibility of a writing center with your colleagues, consider the following framework questions:

- How does the writing center fit into your curricular goals and objectives?
- What learning objectives are fulfilled through the students' work in the writing center? (Many of the Common Core State Standards for writing or writing standards from other states can be met with writing center pedagogy, and these standards are discussed in the lesson plans in Chapter 6.) Also consider cross-curricular connections such as students' ability to ask open-ended questions and pose and solve problems in math and science; content area writing support and development; and engaging students in authentic inquiry.
- What else do you want students to get out of their writing center experiences?
- Do you have a strong vertical integration across grade levels? What types of vertical integration or collaboration will be needed for your writing center model?
- Do you have departmentalized subject instruction for the upper grades? How does this affect who will teach the writing center lessons and direct the writing center? How does this affect the schedule of the writing center?
- What resources might you need?

Write your answers down. Create a matrix to show the learning objectives that will be met, or draw a diagram to illustrate the framework of your writing center. Use this visual as you continue to discuss the framework for your writing center.

FIGURING OUT THE INSTRUCTIONAL LOGISTICS

In addition to thinking over the questions listed above, you will need to consider who will lead the writing center tutor training lessons, along with a couple of other important instructional logistic concerns:

- Who will teach the writing center tutor training lessons? You may need one teacher per grade level (if tutors are from multiple grade levels) to teach the tutor lessons, or you may want all the teachers in the tutoring grade to teach them. If you have a departmentalized structure for subject area instruction, you might have just the writing teacher teach the tutor lessons.

- How much time do you want to spend on the training cycle? Do you want to teach one topic a week for 8 weeks? (The lessons are designed to take approximately two instructional sessions a week, for 8 weeks.) Or do you want to teach them in a shorter or longer time frame?
- Who will facilitate the writing center? In other words, who will supervise and coach the students during their peer tutoring sessions? It could be someone other than the director.

If the person teaching the tutor training lessons is not the writing center facilitator/supervisor, you'll need to make sure that the supervisor is thoroughly familiar with those lessons so that there can be continuity among teachers and writing center facilitators. In addition, it is important to make sure that all of the teachers involved read and discuss Chapters 2 and 3 so that everyone is operating from the same theoretical framework. We know we're a little biased, but it would truly be beneficial if all the participating teachers (the teachers sending students to the writing center, the writing center supervisor, and the one[s] teaching the tutor training lessons) read this book. It will help begin important conversations about how to best support your writers and how to continue to grow your practice as a writing teacher. It will also help everyone understand the scope of the writing center along with the writing process and writing center principles that guide this instruction. Change happens most effectively when people share a vision, understand the goals and objectives of the work, and have common strategies for getting there.

THE PHYSICAL SPACE

While the act of tutoring itself takes little space, there are questions to consider and decisions to be made regarding the writing center space: Do you have a separate space to house the writing center? Is there a space that is semi-occupied, such as the library media center or some other common space, that would be able to double as the writing center? Will the writing center be located in a particular classroom? Or will it rotate between two or three teachers' rooms throughout the year? Your decisions about where to house the writing center will be influenced by who the supervisor is, how often your writing center is open, and the various instructional schedules involved.

Here are some space configurations we suggest:

- Writing center in the library or other central location
- Writing center in a rotating classroom
- Writing center in a stationary classroom

If the writing center is located in the library, the librarian may or may not be able to assist with the session supervision; this is something you'll want to discuss with colleagues. You will also need to make sure that the writing center doesn't interrupt the librarian's classes. Is there a regular time when the library isn't being used for library class sessions? If the library is too much of a bustling, busy space throughout the day, you may want to find another central location. If your school has an atrium, nice outdoor space with tables, central cafeteria, or other common area, you may want to use that space.

The physical writing center and the supervision could rotate between multiple teachers. For example, if the 4th-grade team has four teachers who teach in a departmentalized structure (one teacher teaches math, another does social studies and science, etc.), they could each take a 9-week quarter during which he or she would be the writing center supervisor. The writing center would potentially be housed in the supervisor's classroom for that grading quarter, and rotate to another teacher's room the next quarter. One advantage of this model is that each teacher has the opportunity to watch the writing center and the students in action. Each teacher is able to take the lead as supervisor, to coach students, and to learn from them as well. We learn so much by watching the tutors and writers in action.

The advantage to having the writing center located in one constant space is that writers know where to go. The students from other grades and or classes who come to the center will become familiar with the space, and it will become a known location in the school. Teachers will always know where to send students when the writing center is stationary, and students will know how to get there. However, if the constant space is a regular classroom (as opposed to a central location such as the library), only one teacher might be able to supervise the tutoring sessions. This arrangement may be fine with everyone, but maybe not; other teachers may want to see the writing center come to fruition and to be able to teach and learn in the writing center as well. If it is in a stationary classroom, it is possible that the *teachers* could rotate, and not the classroom. So the supervising teacher would move to the writing center room for that period, and his or her students would stay put (with another teacher coming in to facilitate independent reading and writing time, for example). This would allow writing center visitors to have a constant location but give different teachers an opportunity to supervise the writing center each quarter.

Again, any one of these might work well in any particular school depending on the school system, stakeholders, and curriculum. One additional space issue you need to address is the number of tutor-writer pairs you allow in each session. You will likely need to limit the number of tutor-writer pairs in the writing center each day/session, according to the space you have available. Both when our writing centers were housed in a library media center and when they were housed in a regular teacher's classroom, we limited the number of tutor-writer pairs to a maximum of 12 per session. This equals 24 students in the room, and that's plenty of students to have conferencing in one room.

DESIGNING AND STAFFING THE WRITING CENTER

Although the writing center itself is organized and managed by adults (teachers or faculty), students lead the tutoring sessions. We therefore choose to highlight this structure with the label of *student-led writing center*. In order to establish a student-led writing center, there are questions you should ask about who your peer tutors will be and how the tutors', writers', and teachers' schedules will intersect:

- Do you want same-grade peers to be tutor-writer pairs? (example: a 4th-grader tutors another 4th-grader)
- Would you prefer to use cross-grade peers, where the higher-grade students tutor lower-grade students? (example: a 5th-grader tutors a 4th-grader)
- What grades are going to be involved? (Who's interested?)
- How can you revise your teaching schedule to allow students to volunteer as tutors?

There are many possible writing center designs or models. In our study described in the next chapter, you will see that 5th-graders tutored 4th-graders. Another year, we had 4th- and 5th-graders tutoring 2nd- and 3rd-graders. Yet another year, 4th-graders tutored 2nd- through 4th-graders. In a different school, a 4th-grade teacher worked with a prekindergarten teacher to develop what they called "writing buddies" using a writing center model and writing center pedagogy. The 4th-grade teacher, Brian, modified the writing genre and traits lessons to teach his 4th-graders about emergent writing and how to support an emergent writer. Drawing upon the guidelines we provided in the beginning of Chapter 3 and his knowledge of Reading Recovery tutoring methods, Brian created some guidelines and procedures for his 4th-graders. He and the pre-K teacher also chose to establish consistent tutor-writer partners, or buddies, rather than having tutors and writers volunteer and be paired randomly. There are many possible configurations, and you can decide what best fits your context.

Volunteer tutors. We feel strongly that all students—*all* students— can and should be given the opportunity to be writing tutors. The tutor training lessons in Chapter 6 should be taught to the whole class. These lessons are really just good writing instruction infused with writing center pedagogy and tutor training. All students will benefit from this instruction. When it is time to open your writing center, simply ask for volunteer tutors. Allowing students to volunteer for tutoring accomplishes many things simultaneously:

- The students who are truly interested and excited about being a writing tutor will volunteer.
- Asking for volunteers limits the number of students who will tutor each session without the teacher having to make a judgment call on who will be the "best" tutor. (If you have more volunteers than space in your writing center, you can come up with a system to randomly choose tutors for that day and save the others for the next writing center session. But students change their mind from one session to the next about whether or not they are feeling up for tutoring that day.)
- It allows all students the opportunity to learn from being a tutor, to step into a student-leadership role, and to be empowered in that role. This is particularly important for

your struggling students—those who struggle with behavioral issues, those who struggle with literacy and lack confidence in their own abilities, and those who are timid in class and never speak to the whole group, among others.

One thing that surprised us the 1st year we established the Skyline Writing Center was that, often, our most gifted students and most talented writers were *not* interested in tutoring. We figured this might be because those students are often called upon for leadership roles and to assist other students, and they may frankly be "over it." They don't feel the need to step into that role again. We also found that some of our most troubled youth, those with unstable home lives and behavioral challenges at school, were often some of our most diligent, focused, patient tutors. So we highly encourage you to allow all students to volunteer to tutor. Even more so, we hope that you will encourage those unlikely tutors to try it out; the boost in confidence, the student learning, and the character development are priceless.

Students who are not tutoring during writing center time. Since there are typically only about a dozen tutors during a writing center session, the rest of the students need something to do and somewhere to work, particularly if the writing center is housed in a teacher's classroom. One solution is to have a common writing instructional time across the classes in one grade. For example, the 3rd-grade language arts/writing time is 1:00–1:45 each day. The writing center would also be open during that same time on whichever day or days you and your colleagues choose. Let's imagine that Wednesdays and Fridays were writing center days. (Mondays and Thursdays could be days for focused lessons, or explicit instruction.) On writing center days, if Ms. Tandy was supervising the writing center in her classroom, any of her students who were not tutoring could be divided among the other 3rd-grade teachers' rooms. In those classes, students would be engaged in independent writing and possibly small-group writing instruction. This way, all students are getting time to work on writing, whether independently or with a peer tutor.

Volunteer writers. There are multiple ways to recruit writers to visit the writing center. Similar to the process of asking for volunteer tutors, the classroom teacher who is sending students to the writing center can just ask for volunteer writers: "Who has a piece of writing that you would like to take to the writing center to work on with a writing tutor?" or "Who needs help thinking through your writing ideas today and needs to visit the writing center?" You could also choose students who you think are in need of a writing conference and are at a stage in their writing process in which they would benefit from a writing center session. A quick way to do this is with a "status of the class" check (Calkins, 1994):

1. Give students 1 minute to think about where they are in their writing process and what they will be working on that day.
2. Go around the room and have each student (briefly!) state his or her status—what he or she is working on that day (what piece and what part of the process). Model brief statements such as "I'm brainstorming ideas for my motorcycle expert book today," or "I'm working on figuring out a good lead for my troll story." The teacher can have a simple status of the class chart, with each student's name down the first column and the different stages of the process listed in the other column, to easily record with a check mark where each student is in his or her process.
3. Identify a handful of students to go to the writing center. You can have students tell you if they feel they need to go to the writing center that day as part of their status check and you can suggest that some students go, based on their status report. Just be sure to make room for self-selection.

While these students go to the writing center, the rest of the class should be engaged in independent writing time for that particular assignment or genre unit, and the regular classroom teacher can be working with individual students or a small group of students on their writing. This structure may reduce class size during writing time while engaging all students in writing at the same time.

Another important question to answer is "How will the peer tutors work with differently abled writers?" Since all students are welcome to take advantage of the writing center, there will certainly be diverse writers and diverse needs. The teacher who leads the tutor training lessons will need to think about different instructional needs such as the goals and strategies for working with English language learners

(ELLs). (Ben Rafoth [2015] has a helpful book called *Multilingual Writers and Writing Centers* that you may want to consult if you work with a high number of ELL students.) Or, for example, if you have students who are deaf or students with dysgraphia (or any other special need), how might your tutors best support these students? These special needs can be addressed slowly, as they arise, or they can be embedded into the tutor training conversations as part of the flexibility of a tutor.

CREATING A WRITING CENTER PROSPECTUS

Once you have the answers to the questions proposed in this chapter, you may want to create a publicity document, or a prospectus, to share with your colleagues, principal, students' parents, or a combination of these (Kent, 2010). The prospectus should describe the following:

- a brief overview of what a writing center is;
- how it will benefit tutors, writers, teachers, and the school;
- a rationale for the need to improve student writing that may include current grade-level writing test scores (aggregate form), the need for good writers in the workplace, or other information;
- the teaching/learning objectives that are met through writing center interactions;
- where the writing center will be housed and who will direct it; and
- how you anticipate students using the writing center: who the tutors will be, how often the writing center will be open, and who can come to the writing center.

If the prospectus is targeted for the principal, you may want to add information about any additional support that you have such as collaboration with a university writing center, a high school writing center, or even support from the school's Parent-Teacher Association to assist with facilitating the writing center. You don't need any of these outside resources to run an effective writing center, but if you have them available, you may want to take advantage of them.

KEEPING RECORDS IN THE WRITING CENTER

An important aspect of maintaining any writing center is keeping records. It's helpful to keep track of the numbers of tutors and students tutored per day and per quarter or year; this information is useful when sharing the impact of the writing center with other teachers, administrators, and community members. It is also useful for the classroom teacher to be able to see which students have visited the writing center. We recommend that the "sending teacher" (the one who sends students to the writing center) keep track of which students go to the writing center each time. That way he or she can see if some students go every time (which may not be productive, because writers also need time to just write) and which students have never been so that he or she can nudge those students accordingly.

Although it is a good idea for the sending teacher to keep track of which students go to the writing center, it is also interesting data to see what tutor the writer was paired with and assess how productive that interaction was. You may want to create forms that the writer, the tutor, or the facilitating teacher fills out, such as the one below.

WRITING CENTER SESSION PLANNING FORM

Date: _____

Tutor's Name:

Writer's Name:

Teacher's Name:

Assignment:

What would the writer like to work on today?

Another type of record, one that is kept in many university writing centers and could be part of an elementary writing center, is a session report like the ones below, in which the tutor or writer gives a brief summary of the session. The reflective process is key to learning and the development of good practices (Fitzgerald & Ianetta, 2016;

Schön, 1984); the session report provides a systematic process for such reflection. Tutors and writers can write a brief reflection on what they worked on that day, what they learned about writing, and the next steps for that piece of writing.

THE WRITER'S REPORT

Date: _____

Tutor's Name:

Writer's Name:

Teacher's Name:

Assignment:

We mainly worked on . . .

I learned . . .

I struggled with . . .

For this piece of writing, the next thing I will do is . . .

THE TUTOR'S REPORT

Date: _____

Tutor's Name:

Writer's Name:

Teacher's Name:

Assignment:

We mainly worked on . . .

I learned . . .

I struggled with . . .

In general, keeping up with the various dimensions of the writing session will help you see patterns of use. It will also help you advocate for continued support and existence of the writing center, should it come under pressure because of limited space, resources, or instructional time. Having usage and impact data is an important part of advocating for and sustaining the writing center. These types of records also enable the teachers and writing center director to look back at the center's use and work to see what might need to be modified or reconsidered. In addition, keeping good records and tracking assessment trends helps new teachers, administrators, and school board members understand the importance of the writing center.

SUSTAINING A WRITING CENTER

The best advice we have for sustaining a writing center is to do the legwork in the planning stages to engage in collaborative dialogues with colleagues, to establish a solid and common theoretical and pedagogical foundation, to develop a clear writing center design that fits your contextual and instructional needs, and to secure schoolwide support from stakeholders and administrators. We have found, though, that major changes can occur in curriculum, districtwide start times, instructional schedules, and administration that make it difficult to sustain anything that is perceived as an "extra." The more you are able to integrate the writing center into the school curriculum, the more it will be possible to keep your writing center going. And the more your colleagues and principal understand the teaching and learning benefits, the theoretical foundations, and the impact on students, the more likely everyone will do whatever is necessary to keep and maintain the writing center. As with life, change is always happening. Nothing stands still; this too is the nature of a writing center. The work, the design, and the interactions will need to be revised and evolve over time as new considerations arise.

Share the load. One thing is for certain: although a single passionate individual can get a writing center started, he or she will easily burn out if there is not a larger network of people who support the work. Because the job requires a certain amount of time and energy, it helps to have a few supportive structures in place:

- Gather a team of colleagues who are invested in the endeavor and will work together.
- Consider rotating the role of writing center director each year so that a particular teacher doesn't get overloaded with responsibility. The fresh ideas from a new director will likely enhance the structures.
- Consider having a writing center director and codirector who trade the lead role back and forth between them each year. This leadership structure will help maintain continuity in the writing center while safeguarding against leadership burnout.
- Delegate some of the duties to other teachers or the students themselves, when possible. Put the students (tutors) in charge of record keeping and positive publicity. Design routines that make it easy for teachers to remember when the writing center is open, when and where to send writers, and so on. See if the central school staff can assist in any way.

Even if you are the writing center director, don't be afraid to share the workload with others. Being the director doesn't mean you do everything. It just means you help organize people and tasks and follow up on that work to see how it's going.

Build a learning community. In addition, we have found that teachers thrive in professional learning communities, when implemented authentically and properly. We recommend gathering the participating and interested teachers in a writing center retreat or professional learning community to reflect on the successes and needs of the writing center as well as to continue to grow your expertise in writing instruction. You might do a book study on a writing pedagogy book by Lucy Calkins, Donald Graves, Ralph Fletcher, Katie Wood Ray, Amie Buckner, Elizabeth Hall, Jeffrey Wilhelm, or other writing process educators. If you have a university nearby with a teacher education program, invite a literacy/writing education professor to facilitate or join in your book study. The more we learn about writing—together—the more energy we have to continue the hard work of teaching.

Whole-class reflection time. Another instructional routine that we recommend all sending classroom teachers put in place is a whole-class reflection after writing center time/visits. Annie Ortiz and Jan Anderson, two of our teacher-collaborators at Skyline Elementary, would gather their 4th-graders after each writing center session (the other students stayed in their classrooms for independent writing time, so everyone was writing during writing center time) and have a debriefing and reflection time. These teachers would spend about 10 minutes having the writers share something about their experiences at the writing center or their writing process. This provided time to collectively problem-solve any interactional or writing challenges that arose. It also provided the teacher with important feedback on how the writing center was working, or not working, for their students and ideas for how things might be improved. If there was a pattern or repeated concern, these student reflections gave Annie and Jan data to take back to the teachers who were doing the tutor training lessons and make suggestions. For example, they might say, "Some students were struggling with what to do if the tutor came up with an idea that didn't fit what the writer wanted to do with the piece. Can you do a refresher lesson with your students on this?" Or, "I noticed students seem to be struggling with the concept of organizing informational writing. Let's each think of lessons to teach our students that will help them with some organizational options." This sharing and reflection time also generated student interest in using the writing center. When writers returned with new passion and new revision ideas for their writing, the other classmates noticed and wanted to take their own writing to the writing center as well. Those 10 minutes of sharing and reflection time were highly productive and served to assess the writing center's effectiveness, provide opportunity for deeper learning, and sustain momentum and interest in the writing center.

Establishing and maintaining student interest. One great thing about the writing center is that student enthusiasm almost maintains itself. If you have students in the upper grades as the writing tutors, the younger students will be watching and waiting for their chance to move up in the grades and be writing tutors themselves. As teachers, we don't want to disappoint the new students or deprive them of such a rich learning opportunity, so we muster up the energy to begin a new year with the writing center in place. Even with same-grade tutors, we see the contagiousness of their enthusiasm: Students who were initially uninterested in tutoring begin to warm up to the idea of being a writing tutor. Writers who were initially hesitant to bring their writing to the center hear their classmates return, excited about their writing and revisions, and decide to give the writing center a try.

As all teachers know, often a peer can motivate a student much better than the teacher can. However, sometimes students need a nudge, as Jan Anderson, a 4th-grade teacher at Skyline Elementary, discovered:

> When I assign writing at the beginning of the year, I often hear different questions and comments from the students. "How long does it have to be? You mean I have to write it more than once? I don't know what to write. I can't write for a whole 10 minutes. Do we have to write very much in here?" The list goes on and on. It can be discouraging. . . . It feels like a huge resistance. When I first shared the idea of a writing center, my students did not want to go. I finally made them all sign up. They had to take a piece of their writing in and find out what the writing center was all about. The response was amazing.

Notice the persistence of this teacher: She didn't give up when her students resisted going to the writing center for the first time. She could have easily said, "My students don't want to go, and I'm not forcing them." Instead, she required each student to try it out, at least once. As teachers (and as parents, if you have children), you know it is important to nudge children out of their comfort zone and try new things (hiking, riding a bicycle without training wheels, eating broccoli without cheese). Jan was wise enough to see that her students needed this same nudge to visit the writing center, and she trusted that ultimately it would be good for them. This is not to say that writing center sessions always go smoothly or always end with happy writers. Do you remember learning to ride a bike without training wheels? Crashing into the utility pole? Scraping your hands and knees on concrete? It took perseverance for you to learn to ride your bicycle smoothly. Similarly, if you persevere through the interactional and logistical challenges that arise in the writing center, there is potential for great payoff.

CONCLUSION

To fuel your passion for your writing center and sustain your energy, we encourage you to get involved in the writing center community. The International Writing Center Association (IWCA) website (writingcenters.org/) provides information on ways to get involved with other writing center professionals, including joining the WCenter Listserv, which is a friendly space for asking questions and getting to know the writing center community at large, culture, and issues. In addition, membership to IWCA includes subscriptions to the *Writing Lab Newsletter* and the *Writing Center Journal*; both are publications that continue to address theory and practice in writing centers. These are venues that help keep writing center folks informed and connected to the larger professional community.

As with all good teaching, your writing center will take on the form and design that fits your students and your context. In collaboration with colleagues, you can create a writing center that nurtures the growth of writers, that supports the leadership of tutors, that encourages the development of metacognitive knowledge about writing for the tutors, and that invigorates everyone involved.

CHAPTER 5

The Social and Instructional Power of Peer Tutoring

In this chapter, we share excerpts of the students' tutoring sessions that we recorded and transcribed. Rebecca and Jenn have shared these transcript excerpts with teachers and teacher educators around the country at annual convention presentations for the National Council of Teachers of English, National Writing Project, and International Writing Center Association, and each time we do, there is such an excitement and energy in the room. The energy comes from our wonder in the capabilities of children. The transcript excerpts give us a chance to closely examine what students do as writers and writing coaches during peer tutoring sessions and marvel at the sophistication and depth of their conversations. Below, we provide the framework for our research on students' writing peer tutoring conversations and an overview of our research findings. (Stick with us. Avoid the temptation to let your eyes glaze over at the mention of the word *research*. We promise, hearing the students' voices in the transcripts and gaining insights into what they are learning about writing is worth the effort.) For us as educators, research into the effectiveness of our practice is vital; class time and students' education are too precious to squander. Research also gives us the evidence we need to advocate for rich, quality instruction.

OUR QUESTIONS

As researchers and educators, we (Jenn and Rebecca) were interested in examining the kinds of knowledge students created during the tutoring sessions. We believe that students' knowledge about writing is "constructed, sustained, and reproduced" through their experiences and interactions with their teachers, peers, and other people

(Greenwood, 1994, as cited in Crotty, 1998, p. 54). Our constructivist theoretical stance leads us to assume that students create both shared knowledge and individual understandings during their peer tutoring negotiations. Therefore, we were curious about the peer tutoring interactions and students' conversations during the sessions: *What did they talk about? Did they stay on task? Were they using what we taught them in the tutor training lessons? Were they working well with their partners? Were they learning enough about writing to make the time invested in the tutor training and in the operation of the writing center worthwhile?* These initial wonderings led us to develop the following research questions:

- What types of conversations and interactions take place in the elementary school writing center sessions?
- What types of knowledge about writing are constructed during students' writing center conversations?

Since we were particularly interested in the student conversations, a conversation analysis research methodology (ten Have, 2007) was a logical research framework. The main goal of conversation analysis is to "discover and describe the architecture" of naturally occurring conversations—in our case, the writing center interactions (Wooffitt, 2005, p. 8).

COLLECTING AND ANALYZING THE DATA

During the implementation of our very first writing center at Skyline Elementary, we audio-recorded the students' tutoring sessions and ended up with 18 usable recordings that ranged in length from 7 to 26 minutes. We transcribed the session recordings verbatim, exactly as they were spoken. In our transcriptions, we noted speech features such as changes in intonation, laughter, pauses, length of silence, and overlapping speech. We have included a Transcription Legend later in this chapter that identifies the marks we used to note these speech features and their corresponding meanings. You will see those same transcription marks in the tutoring session excerpts we share. We used these transcription marks to help us recreate, as much as possible, the conversation and the sound of the students' voices during the interactions. As you have likely experienced with text messages and e-mails, it's difficult to convey the personal and intonation qualities of speech in written text, but *how* we say something greatly affects its meaning. So, we took care to note how things were said to help us understand the meanings and intentions behind the language.

In selecting our analysis methods, we drew upon the work of ten Have (2007) and Wooffitt (2005). We analyzed the conversation data phrase by phrase and turn by turn noting the actions in which the tutors and writers were engaged, the sequence of those actions, the types of conversations they were having, the writing processes the children were using, and the topics of conversation. We also examined the patterns of writer and tutor actions and conversations within and across sessions in order to examine the student learning that took place. As part of our analysis process, we created an outline of the episodes and action sequences in each tutoring session. This outline of episodes (larger conversational units with an identifiable focus or action intention that had a clear beginning and ending) and action sequences (what the students did and talked about) helped us see the overall "map" of the conversation and identify the types of conversations and interactions that took place in the tutoring sessions.

Our analysis revealed surprising and exciting findings. Not only were the students on task for the majority of their tutoring sessions (there was actually *very* little off-task conversation across the sessions), but they were also engaged in rich conversations about the writing and writing process that nudged writers forward in productive ways.

THE STUDENTS

Before presenting the research on the topics and types of writing center conversations, we want to take a moment to tell you about the children. Skyline Elementary, the school that the children in our study attended, serves a high-needs community. Housed in a beautiful, modern, single-story building, the school is located in a quiet, older neighborhood. In the front entry hallway, an aviary catches the attention of many. Skyline is a Title I school, which means it has a high population of children and families living at or below the poverty line and qualifies for special funding and services as a result. Approximately 57% of the students are eligible for free or reduced-price lunches. The majority of the families fall in "working class" and low-income socioeconomic categories, with a small percentage of middle-income level families. The school serves a culturally diverse population with approximately a quarter of its students from African American, Asian, Native American, and Hispanic heritages. The rate of student mobility at this school is 7–10%. The school has had strong leadership and strong teachers, with about a dozen National Board Certified Teachers and a handful of National Writing Project teacher consultants at Skyline at the time of this project. This background information is important because it, coupled with the findings of our research, shows that *all* children can benefit from high-quality writing process and writing center pedagogy, not just those from affluent and ideal circumstances.

WHAT DID THEY TALK ABOUT?
STUDENTS' WRITING CENTER CONVERSATIONS

The children engaged in a surprising breadth and depth of writing conversations and interactions. Their conversations showed how they were internalizing the traits of good writing and enacting the writing strategies they knew. They were doing what writers do: contemplating and elaborating upon details, looking for places to strengthen the piece, clarifying confusing phrases in the writing, brainstorming ideas, drafting, editing, seeking confirmation about the merit of their ideas and work, and gauging the responses of their audience. The conversations were rich and focused, and when we looked closely, we noticed that even the sessions in which there appeared to be tensions between the tutor and writer resulted in productive dialogue.

Portions of their conversations involved the logistics of peer tutoring: establishing rapport, deciding how to start the writing discussion, asking for adult help if the students became stuck, and concluding the session. However, the majority of time was spent talking about the content of the writing and the writer's process. This is exactly what we would hope for! We want writing coaches (whether they are peer tutors or teachers) to focus on the content of the piece first as well as the writer's process, rather than spending too much time on grammar and conventions in the early stages of a piece's development.

Conversations about Content and Ideas. The students talked about writing traits such as content and ideas, genre format and structure, grammar and conventions, and word choice. Below is a list, based on our analysis, of the students' most frequent discussion topics that centered on the writing itself (as opposed to focusing on the process):

- The writer's interest in the topic
- The author's intentions for the piece
- Considering the audience
- Identifying, clarifying, or revising the main idea or topic
- Considering genre and format
- Clarifying reader confusion
- Working on the organization of ideas
- Discussing grammar and conventions
- Requesting more detail
- Brainstorming ideas for new details
- Checking informational accuracy

This is an amazing list! Fourth and 5th-graders were talking about why they chose to write about a certain topic and what their background knowledge or experiences were with their topics. They were asking questions about audience such as, "Will people understand what I'm saying here? Can you picture this part here? Will the reader be confused? Who is this piece for?" They were working together to figure out particular genres and genre parameters: mystery novel, alphabet book, Mother's Day poem, essay, and so on. And they were combining their knowledge of grammar and conventions to edit the spelling, punctuation, and syntax of the writing.

The students also engaged in lengthy conversations about the details of a piece of writing. Tutors often requested that the writer include additional details. In making these requests, some tutors began with questions that included a prompt for specific details ("Is there something you could add about your brother or sister?), or they began with an open-ended question inquiring about the details ("Can you give me a few examples?") and moved to a more specific prompt when the open-ended question didn't elicit enough information from the writer. Some tutors used a combination of yes/no questions, open-ended questions, and prompts for specific details to solicit the additional information from the writers. Since we emphasized the use of open-ended questions by tutors, we were pleased to see the tutors using them in their sessions. You will see examples of these discussions about adding (and even deleting) details in the tutoring session excerpts presented in this chapter.

As writing teachers, our goal is for students to develop as writers. We want them to *be* writers. We want them to consider all the things writers consider when crafting a piece—genre, organization, audience, purpose, style, mechanics, details, word choice, imagery, main ideas, and informational accuracy—and to enact the strategies necessary to achieve these elements successfully in their writing. The 4th- and 5th-graders at Skyline Elementary were doing these things; they were living and interacting as real writers. The peer tutoring interactions provided space for students to simultaneously articulate, enact, and strengthen their knowledge about what constitutes good writing.

Conversations about the Writing Process. In addition to conversations about the content of the writing, students also engaged in conversations about the writing *process*. They worked together to generate ideas for a piece of writing, to discuss potential revisions, and to edit their work. They also discussed how the writer gathered information for the writing, and they reflected on the writer's composing process. The following list highlights the writing processes the students discussed during their writing center sessions:

- Brainstorming ideas for a new piece
- Drafting new portions of the piece
- Reading the piece aloud to check progress
- Reading the piece aloud while composing
- Revision discussions about main idea, word choice, organization, and titles
- Generating ideas for revision possibilities
- Revising to add more detail to a piece
- Debating a particular revision
- Inquiring about the spelling of a word
- Editing for spelling and mechanics
- Reflecting on the writer's process
- Discussing the writer's history as a writer
- Considering ways to publish or share the work
- Discussing challenges the writer is facing with the piece or with writing in general
- Revealing intertextual connections the writer was making to something else he or she had previously read or written

It is impossible to separate writing products from the processes used to create them. So our separate lists of what the students talked about— the first list of the traits or content of the writing and the second list of writing processes—clearly have connections and overlap between them.

In addition to the discussion topics and tutoring actions listed above, the tutors had to improvise and negotiate the unique and sometimes unexpected needs of writers. Some writers brought unfinished drafts or came with just a beginning idea for a piece and drafted during the tutoring session; this created a phenomenon of silence, and the tutors had to figure out what to do during the silent writing time. We had not trained tutors to deal with a writer's need for quiet time to write, but the tutors handled this obstacle intuitively. Some tutors waited patiently at the table while the writers drafted; others adeptly told the writer they would return after a little while and got up to walk around the library, giving the writer space to think and write. Some tutors struggled with the silence and could barely stand the quiet. Hindsight shows us that this is an area we can address, as teachers, during the tutor training lessons and discussions.

One of the things we found particularly noteworthy was that students' writing conversations focused heavily on the details of the writing—adding, clarifying, or brainstorming details—and the majority of the conversations were discussions about revision. This was likely because the tutors had been trained to focus first on content and idea development and organization of the writing. We saw several instances of tutors taking time to search for something that needed to be improved in the writing and working to frame a relevant question for the writer. There were also several instances of tutors asking the writers to talk about their topic: "What'd you write about?" or "How did you break your foot?" or "Can you tell me more about that?" These types of questions got the writer to talk about his or her topic and elaborate on the ideas. Often, those verbalized ideas became new details in the writing.

There were times when the revision conversations were true collaborations; the tutor and writer were co-constructing ideas and building on each other's suggestions. You will see this happen in the first tutoring session excerpt with Jason and Selena below. Other times, the tutors initiated the revision discussion and had to work to maintain that line of conversation. Tutors who were more successful in getting the writer to consider revision were ones who continued trying different questions until one resonated and the writer took up the revision discussion, elaborating on the ideas of the piece and explaining how he or she could include new ideas in the text. Successful revision conversations often ended with an agreement between the tutor and the writer that the new ideas were suitable and acknowledgment of ways to revise the piece.

The revision conversations didn't always go so smoothly, however. As you will see in the tutoring session excerpts below, some writers were particularly resistant to revision. These writers refused to take up a revision idea or they rejected the tutor's revision suggestions. (In some ways, we were happy to see this type of writer autonomy.) One writer (Scott, in the second excerpt below) refused nearly every suggestion his tutor made, each time asserting his decision with an explanation of his intentions for that section of writing. Another writer refused to consider the tutor's suggestions by either ignoring the tutor's comments completely or by giving curt "no" responses without any explanation or elaboration of her ideas. Typically, the tutors conceded to the writer and either tried a different angle to communicate their suggestion or changed the focus of the session to another topic. (We were actually pleased to see the tutors defer to the writer's wishes, because one of the philosophies of writing centers is that the writer should maintain control of his or her piece, not the tutor.) In one case, the tutor moved to working on more surface level issues of conventions because that was more neutral, uncontested ground; perhaps editing for conventions felt easier for the writer to accept than revision suggestions for ideas to which the writer may have felt a strong personal connection. We argue, however, that even these contested revision suggestions led to productive conversation between the coach and creator (a.k.a. tutor and writer). The processes of the writers *considering* revision and articulating his or her intentions for the piece are very important skills for writers. Even if the student didn't actually make any changes to the text, the opportunity to think through—verbally and in collaboration with a peer—his or her intentions for the text benefits the writer, and the stance of being open to revision (if not now, then in the future) is crucial to being a strong writer.

Teachers have often struggled with how to motivate writers to revise their work and how to support them in making meaningful revisions. Having a real reader, a peer, ask questions about the content of the writing or make requests for additional information provided writers with the motivation to make changes to their writing. A real audience and peer feedback was highly motivating for many students. Revision is at the heart of writing center work; it's at the heart of good writing. We were thrilled to see students so deeply immersed in meaningful and substantive revision conversations during their writing center collaborations.

Next, we turn to the students' writing center conversations. The tutoring session excerpts in the following section provide an opportunity for you to hear the students in action and to marvel with us at their brilliance.

LISTENING IN ON THE TUTORING SESSIONS

You stuck with us through the research findings (thanks!), and now we're at the fun part—listening to the students. The tutoring session excerpts we present here involve students negotiating revision conversations and discussions about details. All student names are pseudonyms. The first name listed in the episode heading is the tutor; the second name is the writer.

As you read these three episodes, make notes in the margins about what you notice the students doing as writers, as collaborators, and as peer tutors. *What is the tutor doing? How? What is the writer doing? Where are they successful in their collaboration and in moving either the writer or the writing (or both) forward? Why is this a successful exchange of ideas? What challenges arise in these interactions?* After each episode, we will share what stood out to us as writing teachers and researchers, and you can compare your own observations and notes to ours.

Jason and Selena's Tutoring Session. Jason was a regular at the writing center. He enjoyed working with others on their writing, although he said that writing was not his favorite subject. Selena was working on a suspense story about a diary the main character found. Jason began the session by reading Selena's piece aloud, and Selena clarified any words he had a hard time deciphering (because of handwriting). Selena and Jason were working on the following section of the story: "It [the diary] was an old one, too. The ink was coming off. The edges were torn. All I could make out was, '*We're coming to the end. Your friend, about to die . . .*'" Selena commented on the "scary ending" and said that she was still working on the story. Then, Jason asked an open-ended question to begin the revision conversation:

J: Is there anything that you could, you think you might be able to add to it? To make it, like . . .

TRANSCRIPTION LEGEND

The following transcription marks were used to note the ways students spoke and the particular speech features we heard that influenced students' meanings:

=	The speech of the two individuals was latched very closely together and there was essentially no pause between the speakers' turns.
::	The speaker stretched out the sound of the word immediately before the colon. Multiple colons are used to indicate the length the sound was held; two colons represent a long sound-stretch, approximately equal to 1 second.
( )	The speaker made a slight pause, less than 1 second
((# secs))	The number of seconds of silence between speech utterances.
((actions))	A paralinguistic feature: laughter, sighing, writing, and so on.
[ ]	Overlapping conversation; the portion of each turn that was spoken simultaneously is typed directly below the coinciding speech.
↑	A rise in the pitch of the speaker's voice, often indicating a questioning intonation.
< >	An increase and decrease, respectively, in the volume of the speaker's voice.
underline	The speaker was reading the writing out loud.
bold	The speaker emphasized the word(s) in bold.

S: I mean, I know I'd want to add . . . more, to:, the s:to↑ry, but
   [like where it says
J: like] more details or stuff=
S: Yeah, like I couldn't, put there was an envelope slipped into the notebook. I mean, I kind of feel like I might wanna word that:, so that it seems:, mor:e intense as we're starting to read it>.
J: <Is there anything you think you could add after that part? That would like, make it more interesting?
S: Yeah: probably . . .
J: Like, maybe what it said, and stuff?
S: Um-hm↑. Like write ( ) what it said right after that?
J: Yeah, like [what the, what the thing said

S: cause I have, I already have that,] but that's at the very end, because=

J: =or like what was in the diary, like what words was wroten in the diary, or stuff like that.

S: I th:ink I have that over he:re. ((2 sec)) Hm. Oh yeah, see, right there, and, ch-

J: That was **it**? In the diary. That's all that's in the diary?

S: Well on the first page, ye:s:.

J: ((1 sec)) Oh. ((4 sec)) Um, let's see. ((3 sec)) What I think is like, maybe if you could think of something to add like about the stuff that might give it more=

S: Like some background infor=

J: Pizzazz. [Or something.

S: information for it↑ or something↑.]

J: Yeah. Or more detail or anything.

S: Mm-kay. ((2 sec)) Or I could add one of those things that usually comes at the end and it tells you what, what happened at the beginning before the story takes place. ((epilogue or prologue))

J: Mm-hmm.

S: Cause that would make a **lot** more sense.

J: Like maybe you could add, like what you were doing before you found the box in the attic. Like how you got up into the attic.

S: And why I was there in the first place.

J: Yeah.

S: That was just a quickwrite we were doing in class, and so, that's what I thought to do↑, but, yeah, I think that would be a pretty good idea 'cause, I have to have something that leads you into there, so, yeah.

J: And maybe if you'd want to, you could a-, you could maybe if you had more chapters after this, like you could probably turn this into a book.

S: Yeah, that's, that's kind of what my plan was. I was thinking ((chuckling)) of making it a nine-chapter book, with a scary ending.

J: **M**:ystery::

What did you notice the students doing as writers in this episode? What writing skills were they using? What Common Core State Standards (see Chapter 6) are being enacted in their work?

The students in this tutoring session were involved in collaboration at its best. The writer and the tutor came together as co-constructors of meaning and of the actual writing. This worked only because the writer was open to this sort of co-construction. One conversational strategy these two students used in their collaboration was the repetition of the other person's words. They each take up each other's words and then elaborate on the idea, moving it forward. The conversation is truly dialogic—a back-and-forth co-creation of meaning. We have bolded the words or phrases that demonstrate this dialogic collaboration:

J: Is there anything that you could, you think you might be able **to add to it**? To make it, like . . .

S: I mean, I know I'd **want to add . . . more**, to:, the s:to↑ry, but [like where it says

J: **like more details** or stuff=

S: Yeah, like I couldn't, put there was an envelope slipped into the notebook. I mean, I kind of feel like **I might wanna word that:, so that it seems:, mor:e intense** as we're starting to read it>.

J: <Is there anything you think you could **add** after that part? That would like, make it **more interesting**?

S: Yeah: probably . . .

J: Like, **maybe what it said, and stuff**?

S: Um-hm↑. **Like write ( ) what it said right after that**?

J: **Yeah, like [what the, what the thing said**

Jason began by introducing the revision idea of adding more details, and Selena interjected that she would want to add more to the story. Then Selena proposed that she do something to make the story "more intense," and Jason agreed that she could add something to make it "more interesting." They discussed a specific change (adding what was written in the diary) Selena could make to meet these co-constructed goals of developing a more detailed and more intense story. Both the coach and the writer assumed revision was a natural, necessary part of the writing process.

Jason and Selena did so much as writers in this short episode. (The entire tutoring session lasted less than 10 minutes.) They talked about genre and format elements such as the lead to the story, a prologue, and turning it into a mystery novel, all important considerations in shaping Selena's piece. They discussed ways to keep the reader's attention (to add sufficient detail for readers to follow the storyline and to add "pizzazz"). They talked about the sequence of events in the story and worked to make those events clear to the reader, considering a prologue (although they misidentify it as an epilogue). They also displayed confidence as writers. The students enacted all these writing skills and knowledge in a session that lasted less than 10 minutes. *That's* efficient, effective, complex learning.

Dean and Scott's Tutoring Session. Dean (tutor) and Scott (writer) met in the writing center one February afternoon. Scott brought a story about a day that school was canceled as a "snow day" (because of inclement weather). This writing center session lasted approximately 14 minutes. The boys began by reading Scott's piece. They discussed word choice when Dean noticed overuse of particular words. Dean also felt that there were places in which Scott "drifted away from the main idea" of the story and asked Scott if there was anything he thought he should change to keep the story more closely aligned with the main idea and theme of the piece. Scott rejected Dean's probes for revision twice prior to the beginning of the excerpt below. As before, we encourage you to make notes of what you notice the students doing and discussing as you read this excerpt.

D: So:, maybe one thing we're thinking about changing, um:, <u>got on my snow boots and coat</u>, and the part where ( ) you're talking about how you didn't spend your time with friends, would you: want to: reword it, or take it out, whatever's: comfortable with you?

S: Well, I think it's kind of cool, 'cause then it makes the story go on, and how when I go to scho:ol, when the snow melts, and I go to scho:ol, um, I don't have anybody to talk to. But then, one of my friends actually comes over, and we get to go have some fun in the snow.

D: Yeah. Well, I like that too↑. Do, we might want to cut out certain parts, to where it, it's still very close to the snow story↑,

S: Yeah.

D: I think that that might, be good, um:, okay let's see, where does it begin?

S: Uh, where I go to school?

D: Um-hm.

S: Uh, <u>so I did not have a</u>, okay:, but uh:, ((whisper reading)) oh, <u>but then the next day, you have to go to school. So, at school, e↑verybody's talking about what they did, but I↑ did not play</u>

with my friends like everybody else. So I do not have anybody to talk to. But, then my friend Christian comes over and says, "Let's go home," or, "It's time to go home." The snow is everywhere.

D: Okay, um, this so ( ) do you think that ( ) it's needed?

S: I like it because everybody, when they like go to school, I know there's lots of kids that um don't play with their friends, they enjoy playing with theirselves, so I kind of put that as I, me, as I enjoy like playing um by myself. But when I get to school, everybody's talking about how they played with their **frien**ds. So then that day, my friend comes, and he, we go outside and there's snow everywhere. And now, I, me and him get to talk about how we um, we um, got to play outside together.

D: Okay↑. Alright. Well, okay, um, the part wher:e you say that your friend Christian comes over . . .

S: Yeah.

D: I, I like it. I'm not trying to criticize it, but, you may want to re, re, reword it, just. a. little. bit=

S: So, like, say, actually say, so then, um, so where ((mumbling, trying to find the line in the story)), but then my friend Christian comes over, should I just put, then my friend comes over? ((1 sec)) 'Cause I thought if I put **that**, um it would be like, well the writers would think, whoever's reading this would think, well who's he playin' with? Who, who is he having a great time with?

D: Um, where was the, the, right here, the boots

S: Yeah, the boots

D: Would you:, you could say um, my, my friend Christian comes and tells me great news! There is more snow. Or something kind of like that.

S: But, I think of that, I think, the reason I did that, too, is because I wanted to put some excitement into the story, make everybody surprised, so I put, then my friend Christian comes over, and said, "It's time to go home," home, and snow is everywhere! So, like, I kinda like, I like to put some excitement into what I write.

D: Would you want to do, my friend Christian comes and he has great news, like, dun-dun-dun ((in a sing-songy tune)).

S: Well if he had great news ((chuckling)), that kinda, it's like, to me, when I put that, I think of it as a, surprise.

D: Mm-hmm.

S: But when someone comes to tells me, I was like oh, okay, now let's go. But when I go out there, and I walk out, and I step in snow, and it makes me feel like, surprised, that there's still snow here. And to me, it puts excitement into the story.

D: Mm-hmm. ((1 sec)) Alright. Let's see, what else, what else, <u>when Christian comes, everywhere, my boots,</u> ((whisper reading)). Where you say that you get your boots and your coat and all your gear

S: Yeah, well I got that kinda from this story, I read it, my dad read it to me when I was 4, and it was where this bunny, um, had, it was snowing out, and this bunny mom told him put on your boots, and he couldn't get on his snow boots, so it took him all day to get it on, and then, um, he didn't get to go out in the snow. So it kind of made me sad, so I kinda want to reverse that and make it where I put on my snow boots and I, and make it exciting.

D: Well, just out of curiosity, see, you did that part up here. Would you want to change one of them from the first, or like you could say, and then I put on my snow gear, yet again, for the snow, or something like that?

S: Uh, here, well I'll tell you something. I've written this story, like, more than once. I wrote it when I was in second [grade]. I did tried, tried, the same thing with it. And I learned from what I did bad, and then I did it in third [grade], and I messed up a little. Then I did it here, and I think I, I got, I like it how, I like it mainly how it is. The only part that you said that should be changed, is um the school, it kinda takes it away, but then it brings the excitement back into the readers, who are reading it.

D: Yeah.

S: But yeah, I could change the um, the second time I put on my boots and coat

D: Yeah. Would the school part, um, I like it, but it just, it lasts a very long time, so you may wanna cut out all the stuff that isn't really needed and get all the information right there, without making it sound like literally listing the things of information and put some, excitement into it, like you said.

S: Well, yeah, I get that but I liked it because . . .

This was such an interesting exchange of ideas, although the session didn't go as smoothly as Jason and Selena's. Scott contested most of the suggestions Dean offered. Throughout this episode, Dean was trying to help Scott see where the story "digressed," as Dean explained to Jenn in a debriefing discussion. Scott, however, wasn't really interested in revising his story, because, as he stated, he has worked on this story for the past 3 years—writing a version of it in 2nd, 3rd, and now 4th grade—and has shaped it the way he likes it. Scott was deeply invested in this piece. Each time Dean proposed a revision idea, Scott rejected the idea by stating his reasoning for that particular writing decision. Although we could view this session as unsuccessful based on the amount of revision that resulted, we could also view it as an opportunity for Scott to articulate his intentions as a writer. Writer intentions can be such a vague topic for young writers to conceptualize and work with, but Scott was clearly forefronting his intentions in this conversation. This tutoring session was also successful in getting Scott to *consider* revision, even if he didn't actually make any changes to the piece. The stance of being open to revision is crucial to the success of a writer, and while Scott is not fully open to revision yet, we can see him moving toward that stance during this session.

In addition to talking about possible revisions, word choice, main idea, theme, and writer's intentions, Dean and Scott touched upon Scott's writing process for this piece and aspects of intertextuality. Writers draw upon their experiences, the world around them, and other texts for ideas and inspiration for their writing. The presence or echoes of other texts in a writer's piece is called *intertextuality*. Scott explained the intertextuality present in his writing: He described a childhood story that had an unhappy ending and how he was purposefully drawing upon that story and creating the happy ending he desired. Some teachers might consider this type of "borrowing" to be cheating or plagiarism. It's not. This is an authentic writing process and a natural part of creativity. An idea is rarely completely new, uninfluenced by past ideas or by the world around us (Bakhtin, 1986). The same is true for writing. Writers build upon their knowledge of texts in a particular genre as well as specific texts they have read. Think of all the parodies and fractured fairy tales that are published. As long as the writer is not copying a text wholly in a way that constitutes plagiarism, we give young writers a lot of latitude in their borrowing or in their process of taking inspiration from another story (television story, anime, literature, etc.). It is actually quite sophisticated of Scott to be conscious of this intertextuality in his writing and to articulate it.

As a coach, Dean was also doing amazing work. He was able to hone in on the major problem of Scott's story—that it seemed to diverge from its theme in a couple of places. Dean was able to locate a couple of specific places in the story where he felt the events strayed from the theme and tried to explain to Scott how those events didn't seem to go with the main story line. Although Dean didn't use the words *theme* or *cohesion* (he said "main idea" instead), he was working with these concepts. Developing and maintaining a theme in writing (and identifying a theme in reading) as well as writing a cohesive piece that maintains focus on the theme(s) are important and complex writing skills. These skills are also highlighted in the Common Core State Standards Anchor Standard 4: "Produce clear and coherent writing in which the development and organization are appropriate to task, purpose, and audience." Students work on these skills throughout their school careers, and writers grapple with these issues continuously. Yet these *4th- and 5th-graders* were having extended conversations about theme and cohesion.

DeShawn and Lena's Tutoring Session. Lena, a 4th-grader, brought her *Wacky Substitute Alphabet Book* to the writing center and was paired up with DeShawn as her peer tutor. From the beginning of the session, Lena met DeShawn with resistance and what we perceived to be a bit of an attitude. We were not sure why Lena took this stance toward DeShawn, but based on their behaviors we speculate that the two knew each other, in or out of school, and had some history with each other. Maybe they've been in the same class since kindergarten; maybe they went to the same church; we don't know. But we noticed the tension. DeShawn opened the session by asking Lena to take out a piece of writing that she wanted to work on, and Lena said, "I already pulled out the writing." DeShawn seemed unfazed by Lena's curt reply and continued:

D: Mm-'kay. ((4 sec)) Can I see your paper?
L: W:hy:?
D: I need to look at it. ((3 sec)) Where's the beginning at? Right here?
L: No.
D: Right here?
L: No: ((papers rustling)) ((21 sec))
D: Okay. Um, ((8 sec)), um, does this need to be in there, 'cause, um ( ) Do you like wanna change this word ((3 sec)) *witch* to . . .

L: No.

D: Okay. <u>She won't let you call her Coach Albertusky when she's subbing in the PE room. Only Ms. Albertusky. Barry Bonds</u> . . . ((mumble reading through the paper quickly)) <u>Mister, is 1,000 years old. He'll turn off the lights and take a sip for squirrel's brains juice, and he looks like</u> . . .

L: <u>Ebenever</u> . . . I **can't** say it right.

D: Evenever, Ebenever:=

L: <u>Scrooge</u>.

D: Scrooge. Ebenever Scrooge. 'Kay. It's a good one. Um, ((2 secs)) ((mumbles)) ((whispers:)) Let me ask you some questions. ((looks at his Question Chart)) How can you make that more clear?

L: What do you mean?

D: Make it where people can understand?

L: He's a movie character.

D: Oh. Okay. ((6 secs)) Can you give me an example of what he does?

L: He's a guy who doesn't believe in Christmas, and he's scary looking.

D: Okay, um ((papers rustling))

L: No, not on the back.

D: Is this the whole story right here? 'Kay. ((4 sec)) 'Kay, uh:, ((paper rustling; checking his tutor Question Chart)) What is most important about E:ban-ver, Ebanver Scrooge?

L: I'm just comparing the actual person [to him.

D: to him], okay. That's good. ((2 sec)) Wanna let's look at a different story?

The tutoring session lasted approximately 11 minutes. In this episode, you see DeShawn identify a problematic place in Lena's writing—the part about Ebenezer Scrooge—and work very diligently to help her fix it. Despite Lena's attempts to shut down the interaction between herself and DeShawn, DeShawn persists with a relevant line of questioning that could help her clarify the confusion. The questions he uses are directly from the Content and Ideas Question Chart (located at the end of Chapter 6), but he carefully selects questions that match the situational need: "How can you make that more clear? Can you give me an example of what he

[Ebenezer] does? What is most important about Ebanver Scrooge?" Lena seems to acknowledge that there might be a problem with the text when she says she can't say the name correctly, but her resistance to DeShawn's help blocks her from making the necessary revision to clarify the troubling spot in the story.

Despite the tensions between Lena and DeShawn, this tutoring session was still a rich and productive learning site for both students. DeShawn identified a place in the writing that needed some clarification and helped the writer to realize that there was this problematic place in the text. Without this conversation, Lena may have never noticed that there was an issue with the character's name and description. DeShawn, through the process of peer tutoring, learned how to ask open-ended and specific questions to help a writer develop an idea. He also persisted in his attempts to help Lena revise this portion of the text, asking her four questions to prompt her in elaborating and clarifying her ideas so that the information would be clear for readers. Although Lena did not make any revision or plans for revision during their session, she left with knowledge of something specific that needed work.

We need to provide you with a little backstory now: DeShawn was a boy who often had behavior problems in school. He was easily frustrated with schoolwork and would frequently have outbursts of emotion when he was upset about something. Many times, DeShawn's emotions would manifest in moderately aggressive behavior toward other students, resulting in more than one suspension for fighting or physical conflict with students. What is so amazing, given his history of behavior difficulties, is that DeShawn repeatedly volunteered to tutor at the writing center. He took his tutoring responsibilities very seriously, never once having a behavior issue during a session. In the session described above with Lena, she continued to be resistant throughout the remainder of the session, and her negative attitude increased later when DeShawn tried to engage her in a conversation about organizing the writing in paragraphs. DeShawn ignored Lena's negative tone and continued, very calmly, trying to talk with her about ways to improve the piece. Clearly, the writing center was a place for DeShawn to shine. It was a responsibility that he *needed,* as Annie Ortiz indicated in the Introduction of this book. And he rose to the challenge in ways that no one would have predicted. *This* is the power of peer tutoring. This is the power of writing centers.

CONCLUSIONS

Even from the brief snapshot we presented of students' writing center conversations, it is easy to see the instructional potential of writing centers and peer tutoring. Our research findings lead us to four important conclusions:

1. Elementary students *can* be effective peer tutors, with appropriate instruction and guidance.
2. Writing center conversations serve as opportunities for students to synthesize their learning in authentic ways.
3. Peer tutors help develop better writers, not just better writing.
4. Both the tutor and the writer benefit from writing center peer tutoring interactions.

Let's look at each of these conclusions . . .

Our research findings regarding the range of conversations students had about writing and the breadth of knowledge about writing they demonstrated during the writing center sessions show us that elementary students *can* be effective teachers of writing for their peers. The benefits of explicit instruction in writing traits and processes and peer tutoring, coupled with the opportunity to discuss one's writing with a peer, are clearly demonstrated in our writing center excerpts and across our data set as a whole. Students worked on the writing elements of topic, audience, main idea, genre, organization, ideas, details, grammar and conventions, informational accuracy, and author's intent. They worked through all stages of the writing process, including brainstorming, drafting, revising (generating revision ideas as well as debating revision options), editing, considering audience, publishing, rereading, reflecting on their writing process, and negotiating individual writing challenges. These writing skills transfer to any genre, any type of writing. These are the skills with which children need to be adept in order to use writing fully in their personal and professional lives.

In addition, we found that the quality and content of students' discussions and the knowledge they demonstrated during those conversations meets and exceeds the learning goals set forth in the Common Core State Standards (CCSS) for Writing. Common Core Writing Anchor Standard 5 addresses the goal of students developing and strengthening their writing by engaging in writing processes (planning, drafting, revising, and editing) "with the guidance and support of peers and adults" (CCSS, 2010, p. 21). Writing centers and peer tutoring provide opportunities to meet this CCSS goal in a very meaningful and effective way. Writing centers and peer interaction also create authentic reasons for students to engage with writing over an extended period of time and do the hard work of revision, as called for in Common Core (CC) Anchor Standard 10. Peer tutors provide a more genuine audience than the teacher alone (who is too often the only one to read students' writing) and contribute to writers' purposes for revising their work.

In addition to writing center pedagogy meeting the CC Anchor Standards for Writing, it also helps teachers meet the Anchor Standards for Reading. Anchor Standard 1 says students should be able to "read closely to determine what the text says explicitly and to make logical inferences from it; cite specific textual evidence when writing or speaking to support conclusions drawn from the text" (CCSS, 2010, p. 10). Reading Anchor Standard 2 says students should be able to "determine central ideas or themes of a text and analyze their development" (p. 10). This close reading is exactly what Dean was doing with Scott during their tutoring session and what all peer tutors must do in order to have thoughtful conversations with writers. We saw Dean and other tutors work to determine the writer's central ideas or themes and analyze the development of the writer's ideas and details, checking for consistency. (This rich learning experience is much more effective and authentic than the typical test-prep worksheet or practice exam.) We saw tutors ask questions particularly when they *couldn't* make logical inferences from the writing, and the peers worked together to include essential details so that logical inferences could be made by readers. Students worked together on issues of word choice (Reading Anchor Standard 4), considering how different words affected the meaning of the writing. Students noticed and discussed text structure, organization, and connections between an author's purpose and content (Reading Standards 5 and 6). In short, they were engaging and *developing* their knowledge of both reading strategies and writing strategies through their work in the writing center.

Good teaching—truly strong pedagogy—will meet state standards and will prepare students well for any standardized test and, more importantly, equip children with skills, experiences, and knowledge to be powerful readers and writers. Our research into students' peer tutoring conversations confirms that this approach results in rich tutor and writer learning."

Our second conclusion is that writing center conversations serve as opportunities for students to synthesize their learning. During writing center sessions, students drew upon what they knew about quality writing and about writing processes to work through new writing situations and pieces. Students pulled together their existing knowledge and built upon it, creating new knowledge during their interactions. Jenn describes the process of synthesizing as "making lemonade." You take lemons (the existing knowledge), add sugar (your own sweet ideas), and create an entirely new product—a sweet, tart, refreshing drink. When a person synthesizes information, the product is original with unique themes or conclusions that the person has drawn from a variety of sources. Those sources are evident in the final product, but the product is more than just a compilation of source information. Working in the writing center provides students with the opportunity to make lemonade—to take their existing knowledge about writing, add their sweet, unique, collaborative ideas, and create new and richer learning than they would have produced on their own.

Our third conclusion echoes the mantra of writing education: "Teach the writer, not the writing" (Calkins, 1994; Graves, 2003; North, 1982). This mantra means that writing teachers should focus on teaching strategies and processes that will help the writer grow and develop skills that will apply to any piece of writing instead of focusing too much on just making a particular piece of writing better. We found that the writing tutors in our study, unknowingly, were teaching the writer, while helping students with particular writing challenges. Dean helped Scott to consider main idea and theme. Jason helped Selena re-vision her writing. Other tutors helped writers think about organization, genre, details, and audience. These writing strategies and skills are applicable for almost any piece of writing, in almost any context. The tutors were teaching the writers, not just the writing.

The fourth conclusion that we draw from our research findings is that both the tutor and the writer learned about writing from the peer tutoring interactions. One might expect that the tutor would be the teacher and the writer would be the learner, but that was not necessarily the case. The tutors benefited as much as the writers did. As seen in our excerpts, tutors had the opportunity to put their knowledge into practice and synthesize their skills during the tutoring session. In one tutoring session (not presented in this chapter), the tutor and the writer shared different ideas for organizing an academic essay. The tutor said, "My teacher taught us to organize our essay this way . . . ," and the writer said, "Let me show you what my teacher told us." Then, they came up with the idea to combine the two essay formats, using parts of each method, into a new format that they liked better. Both students were learning about writing from this interchange, as was the case with most of the tutoring interactions.

These positive results didn't happen by chance, however. Thoughtfully planned, carefully sequenced, theoretically sound writing lessons were taught to the students. They were taught writing processes, traits of good writing, and how to talk to their peers about writing. We modeled how to peer tutor and how to ask open-ended questions. We practiced peer tutoring several times. And teachers were there to support students when they got stuck. With such instruction, the learning is immense. In the next chapter, we share our tutor training lessons and procedures for teaching students to be writing coaches.

CHAPTER 6

Teaching Children to Become Writing Coaches

Children (and most adults) do not intuitively know how to talk about writing with a peer, even if they are good writers themselves. They need explicit instruction in how to ask questions of a writer, how to talk about strengths, and how to encourage writers to say and write more. This chapter includes 8 weeks of lessons that teachers can use to help children learn to talk to their peers about writing and to guide them in becoming writing coaches. Our goals for these lessons are to teach children what makes good writing, to teach then how to engage in conversations about writing, and to help them grow into effective writing coaches.

Many of the lessons were originally created by Rebecca and the Oklahoma State University writing tutors (graduate students) from the OSU Writing Center. As the lessons were used in classrooms, teachers naturally modified the lessons to be more effective. At the end of the 2nd year, the 4th- and 5th-grade teachers—Jan, Annie, Heather, Julie, Carey, and Cate—along with Jenn and Rebecca, spent several writing sessions revising the lessons and writing them in a format that could be easily used by other teachers. The lessons were revised again during our collaboration with the Will Rogers Elementary teachers as they implemented them. So the lessons that follow are truly a collaboration between all of us. One more important note: Since these lesson plans were originally written for 4th- and 5th-grade students, the sample teacher language is most appropriate for those grades. For teachers who want to train younger or older students to be peer tutors, the instructional language and content will have to be modified accordingly. Teachers can also decide whether, how, and when to use or adapt the WRITE mnemonic and Tutor Question Charts at the end of this chapter to meet the needs of students in the lower elementary grades.

The lesson plans are written in a fairly detailed manner. Suggested teacher language has been italicized in the lesson plans. Teachers have told us that they appreciate this possible language as a way to fully understand the content and objectives of the lessons. However, we are in no way intending to "script" lessons for teachers. We highly value your expertise and knowledge of your students and context, and we know that each of you has a personal teaching style and philosophy that will likely require you to make revisions of your own. We encourage you to read the lesson plans carefully a couple of times to familiarize yourself with the lesson objectives, concepts, strategies and skills, and procedures, and then use the words that come naturally to you as you teach them.

The lesson plans follow this general format:

- Length of the Lesson
- Description of Writing Component
- Student Learning Objectives
- Common Core Standards Addressed
- Resources/Materials
- Overview of the Lesson
- The Engagement
- Student Practice
- Teacher's Reflections (where applicable)

Since most teachers designate about 45 minutes for writing time, some of the longer lessons will likely take two or three writing periods (spread over 2 or 3 days) to teach, depending on the length of your writing time and what you choose to do as support or extension lessons in between these tutor training lessons. We have included supportive information in the lessons such as examples of teacher language, student dialogue, or teacher–student interactions, quickwrite suggestions, and teacher reflections on implementation.

CONNECTIONS TO THE COMMON CORE STATE STANDARDS

The Common Core State Standards (CCSS) for English Language Arts were published in 2010. Forty-five states have voluntarily adopted these standards or are in a transitional period of integrating these standards into their instructional and assessment processes. Although the creation and implementation of the CCSS has been a highly contentious and politically charged process, it is not the intent of this book to debate its merits and flaws. Here, we simply address the ways peer tutoring and writing center pedagogy might meet these standards, if the state mandates their use.

For the elementary grades, the CCSS for English Language Arts are organized around 10 central expectations, or "anchor standards," in reading, writing, speaking and listening, and language, with more detailed standards for each grade level in grades K–5. The 10 Anchor Standards for Writing, taken from www.corestandards.org, for elementary students are as follows:

Text Types and Purposes

1. Write arguments to support claims in an analysis of substantive topics or texts, using valid reasoning and relevant and sufficient evidence.
2. Write informative/explanatory texts to examine and convey complex ideas and information clearly and accurately through the effective selection, organization, and analysis of content.
3. Write narratives to develop real or imagined experiences or events using effective technique, well-chosen details, and well-structured event sequences.

Production and Distribution of Writing

4. Produce clear and coherent writing in which the development, organization, and style are appropriate to task, purpose, and audience.
5. Develop and strengthen writing as needed by planning, revising, editing, rewriting, or trying a new approach.
6. Use technology, including the Internet, to produce and publish writing and to interact and collaborate with others.

Research to Build and Present Knowledge

7. Conduct short as well as more sustained research projects based on focused questions, demonstrating understanding of subject matter under investigation.
8. Gather relevant information from multiple print and digital sources, assess the credibility and accuracy of each source, and integrate the information while avoiding plagiarism.
9. Draw evidence from literary or informational texts to support analysis, reflection, and research.

Range of Writing

> 10. Write routinely over extended time frames (time for research, reflection, and revision) and shorter time frames (a single sitting or a day or two) for a range of tasks, purposes, and audiences.

The lessons presented in this book align well with the CCSS Anchor Standards for Writing, particularly Standards 4 and 5 related to the production and distribution of writing and Standard 10, which addresses both brief and extended processes of writing. Anchor Standards 1 through 3 can also be addressed well with writing center pedagogy and practice, depending on the genre studies that teachers choose to conduct. We encourage wide and regular writing and have created these lessons so that there is a lot of space to incorporate wide writing in a variety of genres and through diverse writing processes. Teachers can use these lessons with any genre of text and, therefore, would be able to integrate work with argumentative, informational, and narrative texts, as called for in the CCSS, within the writing center procedures described here. CCSS Anchor Standard 6, regarding the use of technology to research and publish writing, could also be easily addressed during writing center sessions if students were able to work at computers during the sessions. Access to a computer would allow students to learn the software and keyboard skills necessary for efficient revision and editing. Writing center pedagogy provides a structure within which all the CCSS can be met. Of course, teachers will have to target specific genre units of study in order to meet standards focused on particular genres, but a writing center approach marries well with any genre study.

The corresponding Common Core standards are listed in each lesson plan. Typically, we noted the anchor standard, and we also included specific Grade 5 standards where appropriate. We chose to highlight Grade 5 standards because 5th-grade students are often chosen to be the peer tutors. However, students from lower grades can certainly tutor, and teachers should simply consult their corresponding grade level standards, as needed.

Ideally, these peer tutoring lessons are used within a writing workshop instructional framework that includes daily writing opportunities for students and allows frequent topic choice. However, you don't have to use writing workshop in your classroom to successfully implement a peer tutoring component in your writing curriculum. What is essential is that the students write regularly, that there is a safe writing community established among students, and that students are able to feel emotionally invested in their writing and personally connected to their pieces. These foundational components must be in place if students are to care about their writing, for them to be comfortable in sharing their writing with others, and for them to be motivated to spend time thinking, talking about, and revising their work.

PEER CONFERENCING OR PEER TUTORING?

The lessons in this book can be used in two ways. You can choose to implement the entire set of lessons with the ultimate goal of establishing a peer tutoring writing center in your school, or you can use the lessons to develop effective peer conferences within your individual classrooms. We imagine that some teachers may want to adapt the Question Charts to be used as scaffolds for peer conferences. Many of the lessons in this chapter deal with helping students learn to recognize and talk about writing with each other, and students try these skills out on peers within their class before they begin tutoring others in the school. Therefore, a teacher could use those portions of the lessons that help facilitate peer conferences without ever implementing the writing center or peer tutoring components. However, we highly recommend taking advantage of the full benefits that come from teaching the students to peer tutor and manage a writing center.

A TEACHER'S FIRST ATTEMPT WITH A WRITING CENTER: A REFLECTION BY HEATHER CORBETT

Below is a reflection entry that Heather Corbett, a 5th-grade teacher, wrote about her own writing instruction after our first writing center at Skyline Elementary. It shows what she was learning and internalizing about the teaching of writing. Her struggles are familiar ones; they are struggles that many of us have experienced.

I like to have everything all nice and neat and organized and not having this as I got writing going in my classroom was a

challenge and even debilitating at times. I knew that—once
my students had a piece of writing they liked or at least were
invested in—I could get them talking with the "tools" of the
coach. I realized that I needed to just have them write, to
produce, to create—and then get them talking about it.

Writing is hard—it makes us vulnerable—no matter how
"safe" the topic or setting is—our words on paper expose us,
and without community, trust and respect, this will *never*
work.

In so many ways, I feel I have failed in accomplishing
anything in writing. I have wanted to do more writing this year.
Failed. I pushed it aside and practically stopped it all together
after the writing test. That's so discouraging and disappointing!
I gotta quit thinking about it and move forward. So what if I
didn't write as much as I wanted to, or I didn't have my students
write as much as I wanted them to. We wrote. We talked about
it. We reflected. We shared. We grew—all of us. Those 4th-grade
teachers got their students fired up for writing, so I think this
next group of students will push me even harder; they'll demand
it—the expectation is there.

The structure we've talked about for next year will lend
itself to that—having the students travel between classrooms
and having the writing center in our rooms will allow us to
hear the stories of Wess, Dean, and Allie, and that will be all the
motivation we will need. They are the reason we do this and are
forever searching for ways to do it better—for them!

Heather felt the nervousness that comes with doing something
completely new in your classroom. She was part of the very first
writing center teacher cadre, for the first elementary school writing
center that Rebecca and Jenn helped establish. So there were a lot
of unknowns in that process. However, you have the benefit of the
years of experience and trial runs that we have had since that first
writing center along with the detailed lesson plans in this chapter to
give you a possible scope and sequence for the instruction. The most
important lesson we take from Heather's reflection is to trust yourself as a teacher and jump in. Even if all your initial goals aren't realized the first time through, you and the children will learn a great
deal about writing and writing instruction. And next year, you'll revise some components or practices to make them stronger. So let the
fun begin!

THE WRITING PEER TUTORING LESSONS

Week 1: Metaphors for the Writing Process

Length of Lesson: Two 45-minute sessions

Description of Writing Component:

In general, there are recognized and similar processes that all artists undergo, although the variations of these processes are endless. John Dewey (1934) says that every artistic composing process begins with a "period of gestation," and Catherine Patrick (1937) says that creative composition also involves a period of "incubation." Ideas are generated by the creator, and then they must simmer and stew for a while. Creative processes also include stages of imagination, perception, representation, revision, and editing (Dewey, 1934; Eisner, 2002; Patrick, 1937).

In this introductory session, students will experience creative composition as clay sculptors. Students participate in a metaphorical activity to compare the writing process to the process a sculptor might use to create a work of art, with the teacher making explicit connections among similar processes for the students. The script used in this lesson was created by Rosemary Faucette (1997), the original author of this activity, for use with secondary students, and we have adapted it for elementary students. (Permission has been granted from the National Council of Teachers of English for us to reproduce Faucette's lesson in this book.) Teachers can use as much or little of this process and language as you see fit, or create your own natural language for discussing the sculpting and writing composing processes with students.

The goal of this lesson is to introduce the steps of the writing process—topic choice, purpose/audience, drafting, revising, editing, and publishing—and the recursive nature of these steps. Students will come to understand, through the clay metaphor, how being a writer is like being an artist/sculptor, and they will be introduced to the concepts of the creator and the critic.

Student Learning Objectives:

- Students compare and contrast the composing processes of writers and sculptors.
- Students explore and discuss the processes a writer goes through to produce a finished piece.

- Students articulate the roles and processes of a creator and a critic.

Common Core Standards Addressed:

English Language Arts (ELA) and Literacy, Writing Anchor Standard 5: Develop and strengthen writing as needed by planning, revising, editing, rewriting, or trying a new approach.

Resources/Materials:

- Modeling clay for each student. If your clay comes in one-pound boxes, a quarter pound of clay works well for each student.
- At least one pencil for each student

Overview of the Lesson:

- Students will make a pencil holder out of modeling clay.
- The teacher compares the stages of creating a sculpture to the stages of creating a piece of writing.
- The teacher encourages students to "smoosh" the clay sculptures two times to consider other ideas, emphasizing that artists and writers often try out many ideas before selecting one.

The Engagement:

Reminder: Suggested teacher language is italicized throughout the lessons.

- **Introduce** the activity: *Today we're going to make clay sculptures and learn how being a sculptor is a lot like being a writer.*
- **Pass out** a portion of clay for each student. We chose to give each student only one color. This way, when you get to the "revision" and "editing" stages, students can share colors to make changes to their sculptures.
- Follow the **Script for Using Play-Doh to Teach the Writing Process** provided in Appendix A, modifying as you see fit. Replace the word "Play-Doh" with "clay" throughout the script. (Rosemary Faucette originally used Play-Doh for this lesson, but we chose to use modeling clay because it wouldn't dry out, and we liked the firm quality of the modeling clay.)
- Let the kids **explore the clay** and just play with it for a few minutes. (This allows the children to be excited and have some free-form play with the clay before giving them directions to follow.) *Exploring the clay is part of getting to know your material.*

Artists experiment with their materials—paint, canvas, paper, charcoal, and so on—and writers explore the worlds of books, texts, and words.

- **Explain** how sculptors and writers use the same processes. *See script in Appendix A.*
- Although Rosemary Faucette, in the Play-Doh script, recommends that students work in silence, we encouraged students to **collaborate** and brainstorm their ideas with a partner or group. When revising their sculptures, we also encourage students to ask questions of each other about their pieces and share ideas for improvement as they rework their products.
- As they create their first drafts, stress the importance of making meaning and developing a single idea, **the concept of unity**.
- Follow Faucette's (1997) directions for having students "smoosh" and **revise their sculptures** two times (in the end, they will have made three versions of their pencil holders).
- Before composing their final pencil holder sculpture, ask the class to **develop a list of criteria** for evaluating a "good" pencil holder. Write the list on the board. Ask students, *"What does the pencil holder need to do or have in order to be a good pencil holder?"* (Further directions in Appendix A lesson details.)
- As students **edit**, they should be checking details, smoothing out surfaces, straightening up edges, adding aesthetic details—just as one might fine-tune a piece of writing.
- **Titling the Sculpture**: Rosemary Faucette (1997) talks about "giving the sculpture a name." We suggest you call this "giving the sculpture a title" rather than a name, and help students to brainstorm and select an effective title. You might consider the titles of a couple of pieces of artwork that have creative titles and a couple of novels or picturebooks with creative titles. This is a prime opportunity to include a brief craft lesson on developing strong titles. You might show students a few books with excellent, unique titles and talk about how those titles are much more interesting than plain labels such as "My Dog" or "All About Snakes."
- **Share the Learning**: Wrap up by sharing pencil holders and talking about the design and revision processes students used to get to the final product.
- **Quickwrite**: We recommend you have students engage in a final quickwrite to get them to record their thinking and describe their creative/composing process. You might use the following question: *"How is being a sculptor like being a writer?"*

- **Keep the clay pencil holders** in the classroom for another week before sending them home, as it is useful to have them when teaching the second lesson.

Teacher Reflection:

The next school year, Annie Ortiz became an enrichment resource teacher for her school, and she decided to adapt the clay metaphor lesson for the lower grades. She said, "I wondered how I could replicate this metaphor for each grade level without stealing 5th grade's thunder. I searched for metaphors for writing and found some I thought I could build upon." She developed three additional metaphors for the writing process: the paper airplane, the puzzle, and the gardener. These three extension lessons are included in Appendix A.

Reflecting on the new lessons on writing process metaphors she created, Annie wrote:

> These other metaphors for the writing process worked for each grade level. Children could compare what they were doing in writing to something tangible. Teachers said they were referring to the metaphors in their writing instruction. When I went back into classrooms to write with these groups, I also referred back to the metaphors; they served as a placeholder for our work.
>
> It seems in education we are always fixing things that are not working or are somehow wrong. Children get this message again and again, especially in this era of testing. Revision has always been the hardest part of the process for children. If they fix something in their writing, they feel a sense of wrongness about it. Using these metaphors has helped that revision process. I have sat with a group of 2nd-graders and listened as they read their work aloud and asked for different words or more details to describe something they've written about. As suggestions pour forth, I return to the authors and ask if they want to make any changes. They are eager. I have listened as 3rd-graders share their ideas and others ask them clarifying questions. They jot down ideas they might want to use. Fourth-graders sneak across the hall to read me poems and stories. They want to share certain parts, emphasizing that these are "only first drafts." The students seem to have a different stance toward revision now than they did before. I've tucked the paper airplane book on a shelf and stacked the puzzles. I think I will be using these metaphors for writing again next year.

Week 2: Learning to Peer Tutor with the WRITE Mnemonic

Length of Lesson: 45–60 minutes

Description of the Writing Component:

Brad Wilcox (1984) created a peer tutoring mnemonic for college students called WRITE that was first published in the *Writing Lab Newsletter*. We have adapted his to be appropriate for elementary school students, and this chart was our touchstone for helping our students learn how to be writing tutors. (All of our tutoring charts are located at the end of Chapter 6.)

As mentioned in the discussion of writing center pedagogy in Chapter 3, there are several key principles to remember when talking about peer conferencing or peer tutoring: (1) Writing tutors should respect the writer by not writing on his or her paper, and the writer should retain control over the piece; (2) give the writer agency by asking open-ended questions rather than telling him or her what to do; (3) have the writer read the piece out loud so the tutor and writer can hear the rhythm, flow, and intonation of the piece; (4) focus on organization and content first and sentence structure and conventions second; (5) the writing conference should be a positive interaction that encourages the writer; and (6) because talk is central to the writing conference, get the writer to talk about his or her ideas, process, and piece. These principles are explained in the WRITE mnemonic.

The WRITE mnemonic can motivate students to learn about the other components of strong writing. Our students got excited about tutoring others, and this motivated them to learn more about writing and how to talk about writing with others. We revisited the WRITE mnemonic each week and showed students how the newly introduced skills or writing elements fit into the tutoring model. At the end of the tutor training unit, the WRITE mnemonic also served as a summary, pulling together all the writing components and tutoring practices from the previous lessons.

Student Learning Objectives:

- Students learn ways to be positive and encouraging to a peer writer in a conference through the use of the WRITE Mnemonic Chart.
- Students practice a variety of peer tutoring strategies while conferencing about their clay pencil holders.

Common Core Standards Addressed:

ELA and Literacy, Writing Anchor Standard 5: In Grades 1–5, the CCSS grade-level standards associated with Writing Anchor Standard 5 say, "With guidance and support from peers and adults, develop and strengthen writing as needed by planning, revising, editing, rewriting, or trying a new approach" or a simplified version for the corresponding grade.

Resources and Materials:

- Copy of the WRITE Mnemonic Chart for each student (included at the end of this chapter)
- Clay pencil holders from Week 1

Overview of the Lesson:

- Introduce and discuss the information on the WRITE Mnemonic Chart (a coaching/tutoring tool).
- Allow students a chance to practice the tutoring process using their pencil holders as the creative piece. Make connections between talking about the pencil holder and talking about a piece of writing.

The Engagement:

- Students will be "tutoring" each other on the pencil holders they made in the preceding lesson. Begin by **asking students to share what they remember about the writing or creative process** from the preceding lesson, when they made the pencil holders. Help students recall the criteria they developed to evaluate the pencil holders (which likely included whether or not the pencil holder fulfilled its purpose or function, the visual appeal or "prettiness," and the creativity of the design).
- Tell students: *"Today we are going to experience the peer tutoring process by talking with a classmate about the pencil holder and his or her creative process. Get your pencil holder and title card and bring it to your desk."* Make sure students are sitting next to a partner for this activity.
- **Pass out the WRITE Mnemonic Chart.** Explain to students: *"WRITE is an acronym for what a good tutor should do in a writing conference. We are going to talk about each letter of the acronym and what it reminds you to do when you're working with another writer or creator."* Discuss each of the acronym letters as follows.

- **W—Watch for ideas and organization first.** Explain: *"When you first greet the writer, smile and welcome the person. Take a few minutes to chat and get to know the writer a little. Then, set a plan and goal for the session." "When you're ready to start talking about the writing, you should always focus on the ideas in the paper and how those ideas are organized, rather than focusing on the spelling or grammar first. The grammar and spelling are called 'surface features' and they basically make the piece look pretty and make it easy to read correctly. The grammar and spelling are important in the final stages of the writing process, but not in the beginning when the writer is trying to get his or her ideas written and organized."* Make the connection to the pencil holders: *"So, with your pencil holders, should we talk to the creator about his or her creative process and the usefulness of the pencil holder first, or should we start by asking questions about the decorations and attractive details he or she added?"* Guide students into understanding that the surface features (spelling and conventions in writing, or pretty details and decorations in the pencil holder) are only important after the ideas and content are complete, make sense, convey the message of the piece, and are organized clearly.
- **R—Respect the student and the student's paper.** *"When talking to another writer, be friendly and polite. Make the writer feel comfortable. The writer might be a little nervous about coming to the writing center and sharing his or her work. Listen carefully and show interest in what the writer is sharing. What are some ways we can be respectful to the writer and the writing?"* Take suggestions from the class, and point out the tips on the WRITE Chart. Refer to their pencil holders and ask students how they might feel if someone told them to change something on the pencil holder, or if someone actually took their pencil holder and made changes to the clay. Explain: *"You might appreciate suggestions for improving your pencil holder, but you wouldn't want someone to tell you to change it. You definitely wouldn't want someone else taking your pencil holder and actually changing it either. It belongs to you; you worked hard on it, and you're proud of it. We need to respect a writer's paper the same way you would want your creations respected. So only the writer gets to write on his or her paper, and he or she gets to decide exactly what to change and what to leave alone."*
- **I—Involve the student by asking questions.** *"Writers learn more if they are allowed to answer questions about their papers and when they get a chance to talk about their ideas for the piece. When working*

with a creator, **ask open-ended questions** *such as 'What can I help you with?' and 'What do you want readers to understand after they read your paper?' You can also ask the writer to tell you more about a specific detail or event in the writing."* Give examples of yes/no questions (questions for which the person can simply answer yes or no) and open-ended questions that require a more detailed response or conversation. Explain how open-ended questions lead the writer to generate ideas and details, whereas yes/no questions do not solicit rich details or new descriptions. Have the students brainstorm open-ended questions they could ask each other about their pencil holders. You can write these on the board or type them on an electronic board. Keep them posted for use in the later portion of this lesson. *"When you ask an open-ended question, you need to make sure you give the person enough time to respond. This is called 'wait time.' Give the writer enough wait time to respond, before you ask another question."*

- **T—Teach the student to write better.** Explain how students might teach the student to be a better writer: *"Give **one or two specific revision strategies** that might make the piece better and that he or she can also use later on other pieces of writing. When trying to offer a revision suggestion, think about what you do as a writer when you get stuck or when you want to make a part of your writing better. Consider whether that strategy might work for the writer you are tutoring. Explain and give examples so the writer understands your suggestions. For example, if the beginning of the story was confusing, you might suggest the writer try the 'write three leads' revision strategy. If there was a place where you got confused, as a reader, go back to that place and ask the writer to explain what is happening at that point in the story or paper. Also, if you get the writer to talk about his or her ideas and explain what he or she wanted the writing to express, then he or she will probably be able to write it clearer when revising later."* (See Ralph Fletcher and Joann Portalupi's *Craft Lessons—K–8* and *Nonfiction Craft Lessons* for an extensive collection of revision strategies that you can teach your students to use both in their own writing and as suggestions when tutoring other writers.)

- **E—Encourage the student.** *"Point out good things about the student's paper, not just the parts you gave help on. Compliment at least one or two things about the paper to show the writer what he or she is doing well. Respond to the writer's paper with interest, enjoy the writing, and share what you liked about it as a reader. If there was a funny line,* *or a really nice word choice, or a great description that painted a picture in your head, tell the writer exactly what section worked well and why. Remember to be a coach, not a critic."*

Student Practice:

- **Peer Tutoring**: Have students take turns tutoring each other about their pencil holders. Give the first person 3 or 4 minutes to be the tutor, and then tell students to switch roles and provide the same amount of time for the second person to lead. Remind them to be encouraging and friendly, to be respectful of the person's work, to discuss the design and function of the pencil holder before discussing the decorative aspects, and to ask open-ended questions that let the creator tell about his or her ideas. **Students can use the WRITE Chart** to remind them of the important considerations a tutor should make.
- Tell students to leave the creator with **one or two suggestions** for making the pencil holder even better.
- As students begin to coach each other, you should **move around the room** and listen to the tutoring conversations, guiding when necessary.
- **Debrief**: Ask students to share how their tutoring sessions went. What did their tutors do that they liked? What were the challenges in the tutoring process? Remind students that they will get more practice in the next few weeks in talking about writing with their peers and in tutoring others.

Week 3: Peer Tutoring Demonstration

Length of Lesson: 45 minutes

Description of the Writing Component:

As described in the Week 2 lesson, there are important guiding principles and practices for peer tutoring and writing center interactions. One of our OSU Writing Center tutors used to say, "We're all friends here" when talking about rapport in the writing center. The "we're all friends" mentality is crucial to productive peer tutoring interactions. Many of our students have long and varied histories with each other, both in and out of school. We talk to them about respecting each person they work with, truly listening, and being open to suggestions and new ideas. These are not easy skills for anyone to apply, but with proper modeling and guidance, children can be quite successful at it.

During this tutoring demonstration, we model how to greet a new person who comes in the writing center and establish a rapport. We model small talk. We also demonstrate the tutoring process: asking the writer to read the piece aloud; using open-ended questions to get the writer talking about his or her piece, process, and problem areas; and focusing on the content, ideas, and organization first, rather than the grammar and conventions.

We recommend that two teachers work together to do this tutoring demonstration, combining classes, if possible, or using each other's planning periods to visit your colleague's classroom for the demo. The demonstration will work best if you use your own, real writing samples and ask honest questions of the writer and about the writing. As an alternative, you can do the demonstration with a student in the class, with you being the writing tutor/coach and the student acting as the writer who is visiting the writing center. Students will need a piece of writing that they can discuss in this first, practice peer conference. This draft can be an assignment from any subject area, a quickwrite that accompanied a writing lesson, or a draft associated with a genre study. (See the "Resources for Getting Writers Started" sidebar in Chapter 2 to help you and your students find topics that are personally relevant and meaningful to write about. These resources have strategies for using quickwrites and students' lives to help them select a topic and write a first draft or notebook entry.)

Student Learning Objectives:

- Students will identity ways to be positive and encouraging to a peer writer in a conference through the use of the WRITE Mnemonic Chart.
- Students will observe a peer tutoring demonstration and identify the tutoring strategies employed.
- Students will apply a variety of tutoring strategies with a peer to improve a piece of writing.

Common Core Standards Addressed:

ELA and Literacy, Writing Anchor Standard 5: With guidance and support from peers and adults, develop and strengthen writing as needed by planning, revising, editing, rewriting, or trying a new approach.

ELA and Literacy, Writing Anchors Standards 1–3, which deal with developing argumentative, informational, and narrative writing, are met by teaching students to attend to the global text issues of content, ideas, clarity, detail, and cohesion.

Resources and Materials:

- Copy of the WRITE Mnemonic Chart for each student
- Sample writing with both grammatical errors and issues with ideas or content (preferably the teacher's own writing). Writing should be first/rough draft form.
- Document camera with projection capabilities or other digital image projection method
- Each student will need to have a draft of a piece of writing that is personally meaningful to him or her. (The piece shouldn't be edited or polished.)

Overview of the Lesson:

- Two adults will engage in a 10- to 12-minute tutoring demonstration, talking about a real piece of their own writing. The demonstration will model the types of questions and topics tutors and writers might discuss.
- After the demonstration, guide students in identifying and naming what the tutor and writer did during the session.
- Revisit the WRITE Mnemonic Chart to help students identify the behaviors and strategies tutors used in the writing session.
- Allow students a chance to practice the tutoring process using their own piece of writing. Introduce the Content and Ideas Question Chart (located at the end of this chapter) to guide their peer tutoring conversations.

Engagement 1: Tutoring Demonstration

- **Set up the tutoring site:** You will need a desk or small table at the front of the room and technology that allows you to project the writing for students to see. You could use a document camera or an overhead projector for this purpose. If you don't have access to either, you can continue the tutorial without projecting the writing, but it helps students to be able to read the text while they listen to the conversation. (You could also make photocopies of the writing sample for students, if desired.)
- **Greeting the Writer:** Have the writer enter the room from outside to simulate someone walking into the writing center

space. Model how you might greet the person, pretending that this is the first time you have met each other: *"Hi, I'm (name), and I'll be your writing tutor today."* Ask a couple of rapport-building questions to get to know the writer: *"What grade are you in? Whose class are you in? Do you have any brothers or sisters at this school? How was your weekend?"*

- **Starting the Writing Conversation:** The tutor/coach begins by asking what the writer wrote about and what the assignment was: *"What are you writing about?" "Tell me about the assignment your teacher gave you. What were the directions?"* The coach needs to understand the assignment purpose and parameters in order to help the writer accomplish the assignment goals. The coach might also ask, *"Who is this piece for? Who is your audience?"* or *"What do you want your readers to get from this piece? What is the main idea?"*

- **Ask the Writer to Read Aloud the Piece:** The writer always maintains control of his or her paper. Ask the writer to read the piece aloud. (As a reminder, we highly recommend having the writer read his or her piece aloud because of the degree of invented spelling typically present in elementary student writing. When a tutor repeatedly stumbles over reading aloud a writer's paper, it often lowers the writer's confidence and makes him or her feel uncomfortable.) It helps to be sitting side by side so that both people can see the paper while it's being read.

- **Be Positive:** Start with positive comments. What works well in the piece? Respond like a reader; enjoy the piece. Point out funny parts, vivid imagery, specific details that were particularly powerful or interesting, or strong word choice.

- **Ask Open-ended Questions:** Ask open-ended questions to clarify any confusion the reader might have with the content, ideas, or organization of the writing. (Teachers can consult the Content and Ideas Question Chart and/or the Organization Question Chart at the end of this chapter for ideas for open-ended questions to ask, or let the conversation evolve naturally.) Keep the conversation focused on the larger issues of ideas, organization, and clarity. Here are some possible questions or conversation prompts:
  - » *Tell me more about this.*
  - » *How could you make that more clear?*
  - » *Can you tell me more about this?*
  - » *I'm having trouble following the story (or ideas). What could you add (or take out) that would make it clearer?*

> » *Can you retell the sequence of events to me?*
> » *What is the most important thing that you want readers to understand?*

- **Wrapping Up the Session:** After working through one or two issues with the piece, ask the writer: *"Is there anything else you wanted to talk about today?"* or *"Were there any other challenges you were having with this piece?"* When you both feel that you have worked through some ways to make the piece stronger, wrap up the conversation. A good question to close the session with is *"What revisions will you make after you leave here?"*

- **Editing:** One alternative option for ending the session might be to go through the piece and edit the grammar and conventions: unclear sentence structure, punctuation, capitalization, and spelling. This should not consume the session time, however. The writer should be the only one to make any marks or changes to the paper. If possible, the coach should explain why the changes need to be made.

Engagement 2: Naming and Identifying Conversational Moves

- Ask students to reflect on the tutoring demonstration and **share what they noticed the writer and the tutor doing**. Have them describe what each person did, and provide students with a name for each action or type of question. **Naming the action** helps students to be able to remember that action later and apply it in their own tutoring sessions.

- Pass out the WRITE Mnemonic Chart. Give students a few minutes to read over it. Ask them which questions they heard the writing coach using during the demonstration. Reinforce the principles of effective peer tutoring.

Student Practice:

- **Practice Peer Tutoring:** Tell students to pair up with the person sitting next to them. Ask them to get out the writing draft they have recently been working on. Explain that one student will be the coach first, and the partner will be the one sharing his or her writing. Then, after 7 or 8 minutes, they will switch roles.

- **Discuss the Successes and Challenges:** After each pair has had the opportunity to talk about both pieces of writing, bring the class back together as a whole group to discuss the successes and challenges of the sessions. You might ask: *"What went well? How did your coach help you to think more deeply or differently about your* *writing?"* Then, ask, *"What was the most challenging thing you had to do during your tutoring session, either when you were the writer or the coach?"* Take some time to problem-solve and consider ideas for how they might work through that challenge next time. Wrap up by congratulating the students on their first peer tutoring session! Remind them that they will have more opportunities to practice talking about writing.

Reflection:

After we finished the tutoring demo in one classroom, a 5th-grade boy raised his hand and very honestly asked, "But what if you're working with a girl, and she brings in a paper about Barbies, and you really don't like Barbies? I don't think I can talk about Barbies." This was a beautiful, teachable moment. We used this opportunity to explain that the conversations aren't about what *the tutor* likes or doesn't like. They are about what the writer is trying to express with the piece of writing—the writer's message. The tutor's job is to get to know why the writer is interested in the topic and what the writer wants to share with the audience, and then help him or her share that information clearly and interestingly. During one of the tutoring sessions, a boy was talking with a girl about her piece on ballet. He said, "I don't know much about ballet, but my sister used to take ballet lessons." This is exactly what we hope tutors do: find a connection or opening in the topic, even if they aren't particularly interested in the topic themselves, to start the conversation and to make the writer feel welcomed.

Week 4: Content and Ideas—"Show, Don't Tell"

Length of Lesson: Two 30- to 40-minute sessions

Description of the Writing Component:

"What does your dog look like? What is its name? What type of dog is it? When did you get it? What do you do with your dog?" You may have had this exact conversation with a student (or several) in order to try to elicit more-detailed writing. Teachers are forever and always prodding students to "add details" to their writing. But what does this mean? What types of detail might a writer use to convey his or her message? In lieu of playing "20 questions" with your students, teach them a few strategies for adding details to their writing.

Detail can be added by using proper nouns instead of general ones; elaborating on an action scene to include vivid imagery; using figurative language; including visual text (an illustration, a diagram, a photograph, etc.); or adding other sensory details. Sometimes a writer even describes what's *not* there or what someone *doesn't* do as a way of providing detail. It is important to teach writers several options for adding details, and then spend time exploring a few in depth. "Zooming in" on the action is a particularly useful strategy for students. Often, students skip right over the action with gloss statements such as, "We played." To demonstrate how to stretch out the important action in a story, you might show examples of books, such as Jane Yolen's (1987) *Owl Moon*, in which the action is described in detail. Guide students in stretching out the important action moments or events in their writing with the goal of creating a scene or movie in the reader's mind. Heinemann has an excellent video titled *Seeing Possibilities*, with Lucy Calkins, in which a teacher demonstrates this craft lesson of zooming in on the action of a story. Below is our version of an introductory details lesson using an excellent children's picturebook as a mentor text.

Student Learning Objectives:

- Students will use specific details—"show, don't tell"—to describe a topic in their writing.
- Students will support a peer in developing the details of a piece of writing through the use of open-ended questions and peer tutoring strategies.

Common Core Standards Addressed:

ELA and Literacy, Writing Anchor Standard 2: Write informative/explanatory texts to examine a topic and convey complex ideas and information clearly and accurately through effective selection, organization, and analysis of content.

ELA and Literacy, Grade 5 Writing Standard 5.2B: Develop the topic with facts, definitions, concrete details, quotations, or other information and examples related to the topic.

ELA and Literacy, Writing Anchor Standard 3: Write narratives to develop real or imagined experiences or events using effective techniques, well-chosen details, and well-structured event sequences.

ELA and Literacy, Grade 5 Writing Standard 5.3B: Use narrative techniques, such as dialogue, description, and pacing, to develop experiences and events or show the responses of characters to situations.

ELA and Literacy, Grade 5 Writing Standard 5.3D: Use concrete words, phrases, and sensory details to convey experiences and events precisely.

Resources and Materials:

- Cooper, Elisha. (2010). *Farm.* New York, NY: Orchard Books. Or any picturebook or text that uses descriptive language, specific details, and imagery to convey the author's message.
- Content and Ideas Question Chart.

Overview of the Lesson:

- Read aloud a mentor text (*Farm* or other picturebook) to demonstrate how an author uses specific details to convey his or her message.
- Identify the types of details a writer might use.
- Students will revisit one of their pieces of writing to add more specific details to the piece.
- Students will practice tutoring each other, focusing on the content and ideas of the piece.

Engagement:

- *Reminder:* The teacher language included in these lesson plans is not intended to be a strict script to follow. Rather, the teacher language is included to illustrate the main concepts that need to be addressed with your students and to provide examples of how you might explain the concepts.
- **Read** aloud *Farm* or the descriptive text of your choice. (The examples in this lesson are from *Farm.*)
- Ask students to **share details about the farm** that stood out for them. As they share, name and **list these details on the board** (whiteboard, Smartboard, etc.). Start to group the details into categories by type, and create names for the categories. The following table shows some examples of categories and details that your students might identify.

Proper Nouns	Metaphors and Similes	Showing Actions	Using Your Senses
Cat names: Oreo, Claw, Martha S.	"Fields change from the color of milk chocolate to the color of dark chocolate." "The farms are like islands on the ocean. The tractors are like boats."	"The cats swallow grasshoppers and hack them up." "At night, everyone itches."	List of visual objects ("a house, two barns, four silos, some sheds"). The smells on the farm.

- **Identifying Author's Purpose:** Ask the students: *"What is the main idea of this book? What do you think the author wants us to know about the farm? There may be more than one main idea in any book. So there is not one right answer. There may be a couple of main ideas that we can agree on."* Consider and discuss the students' ideas. Ask students to provide evidence from the text that supports each hypothesis about the main idea. Then come to a consensus of the group about the main idea or ideas.
- **Connect the Author's Purpose to the Writing Strategy:** Ask students, *"How do the details in this book help Elisha Cooper make his main point of . . . [insert the main idea(s)]?"*
- **Identify the Writing Strategy:** Tell students: *"The writing strategy of using specific details to express your main ideas is called 'show, don't tell.' When a writer shows, he or she is describing something so that you can create a picture in your mind or so that you can see it, feel it, or smell it. Elisha Cooper is not just telling you he loves the farm. He didn't just say, 'I love the farm." Or, 'The farm has all kinds of strange smells in the summertime.' That would be just telling the reader what he thinks. Instead, he showed us. He showed us by giving each of the cats names and showing us exactly what they do. He gave us the sense of being there by describing each of the specific smells of the farm. You can do this in your writing too. You can use the 'show, don't tell' strategy in your writing to make it more interesting and meaningful for your readers."*

Student Practice:

- **Try the Strategy:** Students need the opportunity to try the "show, don't tell" writing strategy in their own writing. One caveat is it is best if the writing is a personal narrative or on a topic with which the writer has personal experiences to draw upon for details. Have students reread their drafts and underline a sentence or put a box around a short section in which they only "told" the reader the main idea but didn't "show" or describe it with details. (If you use writer's notebooks in your class, you can have students go back to a notebook entry or draft and underline a sentence there.) Then, give students time to revise that section of the writing by using one of the strategies you discussed to add detail (5–10 minutes should be a sufficient amount of time for students to revise the one small section they underlined or boxed).
- **Share:** Have several students explain which writing strategy they used to expand their writing. You might want to have a student read both the original and the revised sections as well as name the detail-revision strategy she or he used. You may need to help students name their strategy.

Peer Tutoring Practice:

- Students can use the same draft piece of writing that was used for the details lesson above for this peer tutoring practice activity, or they can use a different draft piece.
- **Pass out a copy of the Content and Ideas Question Chart** to each student.
- **Introduce the Content and Ideas Question Chart** to the class: The left-hand column has yes or no questions that the coach can ask him- or herself mentally when thinking about a piece of writing. The right-hand column has corresponding open-ended questions the coach can ask to help the writer elaborate on the paper. For example, the tutor might ask him- or herself, "Is the topic big enough or broad enough to write a whole report about?" Then, he or she would move to the right-hand column and ask the writer one or more of the related, open-ended questions: "What is your topic? Can you tell me more about your topic? How can you make that topic bigger or broader so that you have enough to write about?" Explain that, when tutoring, it is most helpful to ask the writer open-ended questions that encourage the writer to talk about his or her ideas or topic. Often, when

the writer starts to talk about the topic, he or she remembers or describes details that weren't included in the writing. The writer and the coach can consider whether or not the oral details would add to the written piece. Tell students that the Content and Ideas Question Chart is *not* a script. It is only a tool or a support for the tutor to use if he or she gets stuck and isn't sure what to ask the writer in order to develop the writing.

- **Pair students up** to practice tutoring each other. Give each coach/tutor approximately 7–8 minutes to coach the writer, focusing only on the content and ideas of the piece.

- **Wrap up:** Ask several students to share what their tutors did or asked that was helpful in developing their writing. Use this discussion as a way to reiterate tutoring strategies that are included in the WRITE mnemonic and highlight open-ended questions that were effective in getting the writer to talk about the topic. Remind students that it is important to discuss the content and ideas in a piece of writing first, and to wait to discuss grammar or spelling changes until later on in the writing process (when the piece is close to being published).

Week 5: Organization

Length of the Lessons: Two 45- to 50-minute sessions

Description of the Writing Component:

Sometimes students will begin a piece with a flurry of writing. They write and write and write. When they finally stop and read it to someone (a teacher, friend, or family member), the writer or the reader may realize a lack of clear organization. The ideas don't flow logically from one to the next, or the piece has four stories in one. However, when writing is organized well, the audience stays engaged with the piece and can follow the ideas to the end without getting lost along the way. Organizing a piece of writing involves choices about how the piece is structured as a whole, how ideas are sequenced, what the focus of the piece will be, how to transition from one idea to the next, and how to maintain a general cohesiveness within the piece. Each of these aspects of organization would be a good topic for instruction. We chose to start with a lesson on common organizational text structures for narrative or informational texts.

Simple narratives, in the United States, usually follow the familiar story structure of exposition, rising action, climax, and resolution. A basic linear story begins with an exposition (or setup) in which the characters and settings are usually introduced to the reader. Next, the action rises and a problem usually occurs. Then, the characters try to solve the problem, and the action reaches its most exciting point (or climax). Last, the problem is resolved, and the story is concluded. Of course, this sequence is flexible! In some stories, the action begins in the first line, and the characters are introduced slowly throughout the story. In other stories, the setting changes from place to place throughout the story. Stories can also have multiple problems or problems that increase in complexity over the course of the story. Some writers even choose to leave readers hanging and never fully resolve the problem. The simple linear structure can be modified by starting with a major event or climactic scene and then flashing back to the events that led up to the big moment. Most flashback stories then continue on past the big, opening moment to continue the action with a traditional action and resolution sequence. Authors may choose to put a flashback/flashforward at the very beginning of a story, as a way to hook the reader, or they might place it in the middle of the story for effect.

Informational texts have several organizational options: cause and effect, compare and contrast, question and answer, chronological or sequential, narrative informational (as with most biographies), problem-solution, and descriptive text structures. In this lesson plan, there is an "Informational Text Structures" textbox with detailed descriptions of each of these structures. The organization of a piece depends on the writer's message, purpose, and audience, as well as the genre of the piece. There is almost always more than one way to successfully organize a piece of writing, and most texts employ more than one organizational structure simultaneously (for example, a biography may be organized both narratively and chronologically). While the five-paragraph academic essay format is one that students need to learn for academic purposes, it is certainly not the only—or even the best—way to organize informational text. In fact, most informational texts are *not* organized in a five-paragraph essay format. As teachers, our job is to teach the organizational *options* students have in presenting written information.

In the lessons below, you can choose between a focus on narrative structure or one on informational text structure. For narrative structures, we have chosen to begin with two basic ones: the simple linear story structure and a linear story with flashback. If you decide to introduce informational text structures for this lesson, we recommend selecting three or four different organizational structures to teach and later, in another lesson (perhaps even later in the year), introduce a few others. Additional lessons on informational text structures might also be taught during specific genre lessons, such as a unit on biographies.

Student Learning Objectives:

- Students identify organizational structures and options in narrative or informational text.
- Students organize written ideas in a logical, clear manner that is appropriate for the genre and author's purpose.
- Students tutor a peer on organizational structures using open-ended questions and their knowledge of text structures.

Common Core Standards Addressed:

ELA and Literacy, Writing Anchor Standard 4: Produce clear and coherent writing in which the development, organization, and style are appropriate to the task, purpose, and audience.

Resources and Materials:

- A narrative picturebook with simple narrative structure and one with a flashback structure at the beginning of the story. (If you have ones that you have already read aloud to students, these are best to use.)
- Three or four informational books or texts that have different organizational structures (descriptive, compare-contrast, problem-solution, cause-effect, chronological, etc.)
- Copy of the Organization Question Chart for each student
- Writing materials: pencil, paper, chart paper, and markers

Overview of the Lesson:

- Using picturebooks as mentor texts, demonstrate a few organizational options for either narrative writing or informational writing.
- Give students an opportunity to work on the organizational structure of a draft of their own writing.
- Introduce the Organization Question Chart.

RECOMMENDED NARRATIVE AND INFORMATIONAL BOOKS

Narrative books with a simple, linear organizational structure:

- *Tracks of a Panda* (Dowson, 2010)—narrative informational
- *Don't Worry Bear* (Foley, 2008)
- *Hello, My Name is Ruby* (Stead, 2013)
- *Exclamation Mark* (Rosenthal & Lichtenheld, 2013)
- *Toad Weather* (Markle, 2015)
- *Each Kindness* (Woodson, 2012)

Narrative books with flashbacks:

- *Swindle* (Korman, 2009)
- *The Invention of Hugo Cabret* (Selznik, 2007)
- *Holes* (Sachar, 2000)
- *The Thing about Jellyfish* (Benjamin, 2015)
- *Pink and Say* (Palocco, 1994)
- *Alexander, Who Used to be Rich Last Sunday* (Viorst, 1987)

Informational books and text structures:

- *An Egg Is Quiet* (Aston, 2006), *Swirl by Swirl* (Sidman, 2011), and *The Story of Snow* (Cassino & Nelson, 2009), along with many other informational animal books, are all organized descriptively. A descriptive text typically has a main topic and several related subtopics that are described in detail. A book about horses that has sections on grooming, feeding, and breeds would be a descriptive text.
- *Oh, Rats!* (Marrin, 2006) has a compare-and-contrast structure in which the author compares rats to people (and other animals) throughout the text.
- *What Do You Do With a Tail Like This?* (Jenkins, 2008), *How Do You Raise a Raisin?* (Ryan, 2003), and *Why Do We Fight?* (Walker, 2013) have a question-and-answer format. These types of texts often have sections that begin with a question. The rest of the section is then devoted to answering the initial question.
- *Island: A Story of the Galapagos* (Chin, 2012) is an informational book that employs a chronological or sequential text structure. Likewise, "how to" books such as *Inkblot* (Peot, 2011) use a sequential structure to convey the steps in a process.
- *Gravity* (Chin, 2014) is an example of a cause-and-effect text structure.
- *Building Big* (Macauley, 2004) has a problem-and-solution structure that is used to describe different physical challenges and the architectural solutions created to solve the problems.

- Using a draft of their own writing, students will practice peer tutoring with a focus on the writer's ideas and organization. (If you are dividing this lesson into two sessions, the first two steps listed above can be done in session 1, and the last two steps can be done during session 2.)

Engagement—for Narrative Writing:

Use any picturebook that has a well-developed story line. Really brief picturebooks probably won't work well for this lesson. It is ideal to use a book that you have already read to the class once before for this lesson.

- **Introduce story structures:** Explain that they will become familiar with two common ways to organize a story or narrative: **simple linear structure** or **linear with a flashback** twist.

    "A simple linear story begins with an exposition (or setup) in which the characters and settings are usually introduced to the reader. Next, the action rises and a problem usually occurs. Third, the characters try to solve the problem and the action reaches its most exciting point (or climax). Last, the problem is resolved and the story is wrapped up. Of course, this sequence of events is flexible! In some stories, the action begins in the first line, and the characters are introduced slowly throughout the story. In other stories, the setting changes from place to place throughout the story. Other stories have multiple problems. Some writers choose to leave readers hanging and never fully resolve the problem.

    "The simple linear structure can be modified by starting with a major event or climactic scene, and then flashing back to the events that led up to the big moment. Most flashback stories then continue on past the big, opening moment to continue the action with a traditional, simple action and resolution sequence."

- **Read Aloud:** Choose a narrative picturebook to read aloud to the class. Tell students to think about the parts of the story (setup/exposition, problem, rising action, climax, resolution) and the sequence of events as you read.
- **Identify and discuss the story components** with students. Help them notice when the characters are introduced and how the plot develops with a sequence of events. List the components, in order of development, on a chart (or on the board) to use as an anchor chart. (Anchor charts are charts that are displayed in the

room and revisited in subsequent lessons or as students need them while working independently.)

Engagement—for Informational Writing:

Select three or four texts that have different text structures. Prior to teaching the lesson, you need to identify brief excerpts of each informational text that you can read aloud to demonstrate the text structure used.

- One at a time, **introduce each of the informational books** you selected with a brief book talk—2 or 3 minutes per book—in which you state the title, describe the topic briefly, and identify the text structure the author chose. Be sure to explain how the text structure relates to the author's purpose or main ideas for the book.
- **Read aloud an excerpt from each book** to demonstrate how the writing is organized. **List** the informational text structures on the board or on chart paper. You can include a few notes under the name of each text structure to describe its characteristics.

Student Practice:

- Give students the opportunity to **apply** the text structure information to their own writing. You can have students draft a new piece of writing while considering either the narrative or informational organization, or you can have them revisit an existing draft to look closely at the organizational structure they used and revise as needed.
- **Share:** At the end of the writing session, lead students in a discussion of the organizational choices they made in their writing. You might ask, *"What was your main idea or message that you wanted readers to understand? How did you organize your writing to highlight that idea?"* or *"Did anyone change the organization of your writing? What changes did you make, and why did you decide to do that?"* You might have students share in small groups and then have two students share out with the whole class.

Peer Tutoring Practice:

- **Pass out the Organization Question Chart.** Read over the chart together as a class. Explain that the left-hand column has yes/no questions that the tutor might ask him- or herself silently while thinking about the writing. The right-hand column has

INFORMATIONAL TEXT STRUCTURES

Students may have already been taught various informational text structures. If not, a genre lesson on this topic will help students coach their peers and also help them in their own writing and reading comprehension.

The seven main informational text structures are descriptive, cause and effect, problem-solution, question-answer, chronological, narrative informational, and compare-contrast (Bamford & Kristo, 1998; Fountas & Pinnell, 2001). While most texts contain more than one structure, there is usually a prominent organizational method for the writing that is directly related to the writer's purpose. This connection between text structure and the author's purpose is theoretically supported by Bakhtin's (1986) theory of the ways in which a speaker's (or author's) purpose ("speech plan" in Bakhtinian terms) influences one's choice of speech genre. An example of the author's purpose directly shaping the text structure can be seen in how Albert Marrin, author of *Oh, Rats!*, uses a compare-contrast text structure for the purpose of comparing rats to humans so as to make rats seem less frightening and help readers get to know these animals. The main informational text structures, as understood from my own reading experiences and from sources such as Bamford and Kristo (1998) and Fountas and Pinnell (2001), are as follows:

Descriptive

The descriptive text structure has a main topic with related subtopics explained in detail. The typical animal report children often do in schools where they research an animal and describe its habitat, its physical characteristics, its eating preferences, and so on is a prominent example of a descriptive text structure. Information moves from general facts to specific details. Authors often start with what is familiar or known about the topic and move to the unknown or new information, perhaps even making comparisons between the known and the unknown. Strong writing will include rich description; just the right amount of detail to give readers a full understanding of the content, but not too much so that they become bored and tempted to stop reading; and skillful use of figurative and descriptive language. Many authors employ elements of descriptive text structure in combination with a second text structure that may be either a larger, overarching structure or a subordinate one.

Cause and Effect

Cause-and-effect text structures show causal relationships between events. This text structure is closely related to the problem-solution text structure and often involves a chronological presentation of events. In order for a text structure to be characterized as cause and effect, this pattern should be prevalent throughout the work and not simply seen once as part of the general plot structure of an informational narrative. Furthermore, in a cause-and-effect text, one action or event happens as a direct result of an earlier action or event; there is a definite (or at least very likely) causal link between the two events. Bamford and Kristo (1998) state that "cause and effect text structures are more often used as internal text patterns within other organizational structures" such as a chronological text structure (p. 34).

Problem-Solution

As the name of this text structure implies, the problem-solution structure serves to convey a problem and the possible or actual solution(s) or both. A person (or group) is typically depicted wrestling with a problem, brainstorming possibilities, and trying various solutions. The difference between a problem-solution text structure and a cause-and-effect structure is that with a problem, there may be many possible solutions, and there is no essential link between a problem and a solution, as there is with a cause and its effect. Stephanie Harvey (1998) illustrates the difference between these two text structures well with the following example. Cause-and-effect writing might look like this: "Goose bumps make me shiver. When the temperature drops below 45 degrees, my skin crinkles into goose bumps" (p. 78). Problem-solution writing would look like this: "Goose bumps make me shiver. But they disappear as soon as I cover up with a jacket or sweater" (Harvey, p. 78).

Question and Answer

The question-and-answer text structure is often descriptive in nature but uses a question-answer format to organize the sections, headings, and content. The question may be stated directly as a question in the heading of a section or may be posed by the author in the first sentence or two of a given section; the rest of the section is then devoted to answering the question, often through descriptive writing. Since developing one's own questions for a text is a reading comprehension strategy used by effective readers (Duke & Pearson, 2002), the explicit questions posed by authors employing a question-answer text structure can support readers in understanding and conceptually organizing the information.

Chronological

In a chronological text structure, the events portrayed in the writing are organized by time, often with the earliest events mentioned before later events. Biography, accounts of historical events, and writing about the life cycles of animals often follow a chronological or sequential structure. Bamford and Kristo (1998) say that chronological writing can convey a "sense of drama and tension" in the story (p. 32), which can be a desirable effect for an author trying to make a historical event engaging for young children. Time sequences can be sped up or slowed down to create drama in the writing.

Narrative Informational

A narrative-informational text reads like a story because it has all the elements of realistic fiction: character(s), setting, plot, and conclusion. The difference between realistic fiction and narrative informational writing is that narrative informational writing is built around facts or real events, not imagination, and ideally has references cited at the end of the book. Authors often employ typical narrative devices such as metaphor or other figurative language, rich description of setting, a chronological telling of events, drama, mood, tone, and other stylistic devices to create an engaging informational text.

Compare and Contrast

Writers often employ a compare-contrast text structure when they want to help the reader become more familiar with a concept, animal, or topic that the reader may know little about. Schema theory explains how people learn a new concept quicker and retain that information longer when we have a pre-existing mental construct to which we can attach that new information (Rumelhart, 1981). Therefore, the compare-contrast text structure scaffolds readers' comprehension by explicitly connecting new information to something with which they are likely to be familiar. Bamford and Kristo (1998) note that well-written compare-contrast texts examine similar objects or features, either whole to whole or part to part. For example, Elaine Scott (2004) employs the compare-contrast structure in *Poles Apart* to highlight the differences between the Arctic and Antarctica: ice versus land, daylight versus darkness, inhabited by humans versus uninhabited, polar bears versus penguins. In making such comparisons, authors frequently use the figurative language of similes or metaphors to make their points.

Excerpt reprinted with permission from the
Journal of Children's Literature (Sanders & Moudy, 2008)

open-ended questions that relate to the question directly to the left. The open-ended questions are ones the tutor might ask the writer during their conference.

- **Point out the two questions at the top of the Organization Question Chart:** "What is your assignment?" and "Will you read your paper out loud to me?" These questions help the tutor get the session started. It is always good to ask the writer what the teacher's directions were for the assignment. Was the student supposed to create a report, persuasive essay, story, or poem? Were there specific directions or guidelines given by the teacher? It is also important for the writer to read his or her paper aloud to the tutor so that both people can listen to the writing.
- **Pair students to practice tutoring.** Just as before, have students take turns being the tutor or coach. You will probably need to give each tutor about 10 minutes to work through the writing with the writer. Remind the coaches that they can use the Organization Question Chart if they get stuck and aren't sure what to ask the writer, but they don't have to use the chart at all. The most important things a coach needs to do are listen to the writing, get the writer to talk about his or her ideas and

organization, and leave the writer with one or two suggestions for making the organization or sequence clear.

- **Debrief:** Gather students as a whole group to discuss the successes and challenges they experienced while peer tutoring. Ask students to share what they learned about organizing writing and what they learned about coaching another writer. Collaboratively problem-solve any major challenges that arose during tutoring.
- **Review** the importance of organizing a piece of writing so the audience can stay on track with what the writer is trying to say. Ask students how their writing became more organized as they visited with and helped each other with this component. Ask if anyone made a big change in the organization of their work based on a suggestion from a peer. You can also review the questions they might ask a person who wanted help with the organization of their work.

Jenn's Reflection: The first version of our lesson plan on organization involved the (likely) familiar sequential writing activity in which students provide the teacher with directions on how to make a peanut butter and jelly sandwich. The teacher follows the directions literally, taking creative liberties with students' vague directions. The result is a messy, messed-up sandwich. The objective is to show students that they need to be clear with sequences of events and procedural descriptions in writing. We taught this lesson several times, and teachers and students alike enjoyed the activity. We even explored ways to deepen and extend the student writing activity. Then Jenn attended a regional International Reading Association conference in which Nell Duke, a noted educator and literacy researcher, spoke about authentic versus inauthentic writing assignments. Nell directly criticized the peanut butter and jelly activity as being inauthentic. Her rationale was that if a person looks at actual recipe directions, he or she will find that there are many steps left out. The recipe directions are not as explicit as we might think they are, nor are they as detailed as teachers might expect of students' procedural texts. So we engaged in reflective practice. We rethought this lesson on organizing writing and decided it would be more effective to begin by teaching students ways to organize their writing. Later, in the context of authentic writing experiences, teachers can add lessons on specific organizational options and structures.

Week 6: Word Choice and Sentence Fluency

Length of the Lesson: One to two 45-minute sessions

Description of the Writing Component:

The books we love and the texts that make an impact on us are usually ones that have creative, powerful, or vivid language. They are texts that have a particular rhythm or fluency about the language that resonates with us as readers. Jenn immediately felt the pull of Ingrid Law's (2008) language within the first five pages of *Savvy*. Her creative word choice and fresh ways of using figurative language caught Jenn's attention right away. It's writing like this—writing that captures its reader—that we want to help our students create. Writers create captivating texts, in part, through their choice of words and style of sentence construction.

In the "show, don't tell" lesson (Lesson 4), we addressed different ways to add detail to writing: showing someone's actions, using proper nouns, employing figurative language, adding sensory details, and adding dialogue, for examples. One commonly overused (and not always effective) strategy for adding detail to writing is to add adjectives. However, professional creative writers often say that good writing is built upon strong, specific nouns and verbs, rather than a string of adjectives (e.g., large, fierce, brown bird vs. red-tailed hawk). Adding unnecessary adjectives or arbitrarily scattering them throughout a text can make the writing clunky and cumbersome rather than improve it. Instead, guide students in replacing common, simple verbs, such as *ran, said, walked, moved,* and *looked* with more interesting and precise ways to describe these types of actions. Instead of saying a character *looked* at someone, a writer might use *gawked, glared, peeked, glanced, glimpsed,* or *stared* to describe the action more precisely. *Touched* could be replaced with *held, embraced, grabbed, squeezed, brushed, shoved,* or *grazed*. Do the same for generic nouns such as *shoes, book, store, car, hat, dog, tree, fish, wind, rain,* and so on. For example, *sneakers* gives readers a more vivid mental picture than *shoes*, and using the proper noun *Converse* gives readers an even more specific image than *sneakers*. Instead of writing, "The girl was reading a book," an author could say she was reading a *novel, mystery, magazine, Seventeen,* or *39 Clues*.

Sentence construction will vary according to the particular writer's style and according to the norms of the genre. In fiction, it is common for a writer to use incomplete, even one-word, sentences for emphasis or to create a certain dramatic feeling. In scientific writing, incomplete sentences are typically inappropriate. In contrast, scientific writing often includes the use of dense and lengthy noun phrases and the use of nominalization, summarizing whole events or actions with a single noun or pronoun (for more discussion of scientific language, see Fang, 2005). In essay writing, some of the challenges elementary school children face with sentence construction are learning how to combine sentences and how to use pronoun referents to avoid repeating the same noun or noun phrase over and over again.

The lesson below has instructional ideas for both sentence fluency and word choice: You might choose to focus on only one of these with your students, or you might choose to teach both topics (in separate sessions).

Student Learning Objectives:

- Students develop lists of specific nouns and verbs to replace more general ones.
- Students describe how word choice and sentence fluency affect the meaning, smoothness, and quality of sample pieces of writing.
- Students experiment with word choice and sentence construction and explore their effects on meaning.

Common Core Standards Addressed:

ELA and Literacy, Grade 5 Writing Standard 5.1C and 5.2C: Link opinions and reasons using words, phrases, and clauses.

ELA and Literacy, Grade 5 Writing Standard 5.2C: Link ideas within and across categories of information using words, phrases, and clauses.

ELA and Literacy, Grade 5 Writing Standard 5.2D: Use precise language and domain-specific vocabulary to inform or explain the topic.

ELA and Literacy, Grade 5 Writing Standard 5.3D: Use concrete words or phrases and sensory details to convey experiences and events precisely.

Resources/Material:

- WRITE Mnemonic Chart (one per student)
- Sentence Fluency and Word Choice Question Chart
- Sample writing for critique (see Appendix B for writing samples)
- Each student needs his or her own piece of writing to use for the lesson and peer tutoring

Overview of Lesson:

- Review the WRITE Mnemonic Chart.
- Students pair up and select one general, plain, or overused noun or verb to work with from each of their pieces of writing. Then, they brainstorm a variety of more specific nouns or verbs that are related to their original word and create a word chain.
- Share several word chains aloud with the whole class, and discuss word choice and quality.
- Students read and critique the sample writing, examining the sentence fluency and word choice.
- Introduce the Word Choice and Sentence Fluency Question Chart.
- Students tutor each other, using their own writing, on aspects of sentence fluency and word choice.

The Engagement—Word Choice:

- Review the WRITE mnemonic, and remind students that you are focusing on processes of "I—Involve the writer by asking questions" and "T—Teach the student to write better."
- **Introduce the key concept** of word choice. *"Today we're going to be talking about how to make your writing interesting by using specific nouns and verbs that help create a mental picture for the reader."*
- **Model the Strategy:** *"Let's start by looking at some examples of sentences with specific nouns and verbs that paint a clear mental picture for us, and some that don't."* The examples below were all taken from children's literature. (You don't need to have the complete book for each example sentence to teach this lesson; just the excerpts below will suffice). The first sentence in each example is one that we have modified to include a generic or plain noun or verb. The second sentence (or group of sentences) has a more specific noun or verb, as used in the original author's work.
  - » Rhodes, Jewell Parker. (2010). *Ninth Ward*. New York, NY: Little, Brown and Company.

    Lanesha and her grandma, Mama Ya-Ya, are talking in Lanesha's bedroom. The grandma gets up to leave:

    "Then, she is gone. *Walking out* with her cane."

    "Then, she is gone. *Shuffling, leaning on* her cane." (Original, p. 89)
  - » Cooper, Elisha. (2010). *Farm*. New York, NY: Orchard Books.

    "A tractor *drives* back and forth."

    "A tractor *rumbles* back and forth." (Original, p. 5)

» Bond, Victoria & Simon, T. R. (2010). *Zora and Me*. Somerville, MA: Candlewick Press.

"Zora and I were sitting under the big *tree* . . . We pretended to be talking and playing with the *seeds* that had fallen from the *branches*, but we were really listening to the *people's* stories and salty comments and filing them away to talk about later on."

*"Zora and I were sitting under the big *sweet gum tree* . . . We pretended to be talking and playing with the *spiky monkey balls* that had fallen from the *sweet gum branches*, but we were really listening to the *menfolk's* stories and salty comments and filing them away to talk about later on." (Original, pp. 1–2)

» DeCristofano, Carolyn Cinami. (2012). *A Black Hole Is Not a Hole*. Watertown, MA: Charlesbridge.

"You deal with gravity every day. You count on it to bring you back to the ground when you jump up. You depend on it when you try to catch a *baseball*, knowing the ball will fall down."

"You deal with gravity every day. You count on it to bring you back to the ground when you jump up. You depend on it when you try to catch a *pop fly*, knowing the ball will fall down." (Original, p. 13)

- **Have a conversation** with the students about the different mental images they get from each version.
- **Explain:** *"These examples show how you can use specific nouns and verbs to help your reader visualize exactly what you want to describe. Next, you are going to brainstorm specific verbs or nouns to replace general or plain ones in your own writing."*

Student Practice—Word Choice:

- **Pair up** the students and have them select one plain or overused noun or verb from each of their pieces of writing. (It may also be a good idea to have some words written down on index cards for students to use if they can't seem to locate one in their own writing. Options might include *ran/run, said, walk, move, see/looked, touch, shoe, book, flower, tree, bag, store, hat, rain, math,* and *dog*.) Then, have students **brainstorm, with their partner, a variety of more interesting and more specific words** that are related to their original word.
- **Create a word chain.** A word chain is a visual representation of related words. The words are arranged in order from least (on the left) to greatest (on the right). For verbs, the least intense

verb would begin the chain, and the last word in the chain would be the most intense. For nouns, you can put the most general/generic noun on the left and the most specific noun on the right. For example, for the word *said*, the word chain might look like this:

whispered—mumbled—said—shouted—scolded—hollered—yelled—cried—screamed

As you can see, some of the words might be equal in intensity, and that's okay. The idea is to put the words in a general sequence from least to greatest; it will certainly be subjective and vary by student. (Some teachers call this a word ladder instead and sequence the words from least to greatest moving from the bottom to the top. For upper-grade students, you can have them choose two adjacent words on their ladder and write out why one was placed above or below the other.)

- **Share** several word chains aloud with the whole class, and discuss word choice and quality. You can even have students write the chains on strips of paper to post around the room.
- **Wrap Up:** *"This is a writing strategy you can use to make your own writing more vivid for readers. It's another way to add detail and interest to your writing. Using specific nouns and verbs is also a strategy you could share with a writer during a tutoring session."*

The Engagement—Sentence Fluency:

This second engagement will probably need to take place on a separate day from the previous engagement on word choice.

- **Introduce the key concept** of sentence fluency. *"Earlier, we talked about using specific verbs and nouns, instead of generic ones, to make your writing more interesting and creative. Now, we're going to think about another way to make your writing strong. Good writing is easy to read. It has a nice flow or rhythm to it, and the sentences are clearly written. Good writers also try to avoid repeating the same word or phrase over and over, unless they are doing it on purpose for emphasis or to create a certain effect in the writing. All of these strategies—writing clear sentences, creating sentences with a nice flow or rhythm, and avoiding too much repetition—are part of a writing trait that is called sentence fluency."*

- **Sample Text:** Using an overhead projector (digital document camera or traditional), show a sample piece of student writing. Do *not* use a student's paper from your current year of students; you can use one from a previous year, with the name omitted, or one from Appendix B. *"Let's look at this sample piece of writing. This writer is having some difficulty with word choice and sentence fluency. As we read it, see if you can find sentences that feel clunky or awkward. See if you notice sentences that could be revised to make them smoother or clearer for the reader. You might also notice some words that are used too often."* Read the sample writing aloud to the class. Have students share ideas about problem areas they notice and ways to revise them.

Student Practice—Sentence Fluency:

- **Apply the strategy:** If you feel your students need additional practice with this concept, you can have students return to an existing draft of writing and reread it with the goal of revising for sentence fluency.

Peer Tutoring Practice:

- Pass out the **Word Choice and Sentence Fluency Question Chart**. Have students read the chart either silently or together as a whole class. Discuss any portions of the chart you feel need elaboration.
- **Pair up students** to practice peer tutoring. They will need a piece of writing to work with. This lesson may work particularly well with fiction or narrative types of writing rather than informational writing, although it will likely be applicable for any genre of text. Allow each student about 8–10 minutes to be the coach/tutor. Remind students to use the Word Choice and Sentence Fluency Question Chart if they get stuck for questions to ask the writer. Also remind students that if they finish before their tutoring turn is up, they can discuss any other aspect of the writing: ideas/content, organization, or details.
- **Debrief:** Gather students as a whole group to discuss the successes and challenges they experienced while peer tutoring. Ask students to share what they learned about word choice or sentence fluency and what they learned about coaching another writer. Collaboratively problem solve any major challenges that arose during tutoring.

Week 7: Grammar and Conventions

Length of the Lesson: One to two 45-minute sessions

Description of the Writing Component:

We purposely choose to focus on grammar and conventions as one of the last traits we teach students. Both teachers and students tend to focus on surface-level components first; it's easier to identify a misspelled word, missing punctuation, incorrect subject-verb agreement, verb tense shifts, or missing paragraph indention than it is to talk about the other elements of ideas, content, organization, word choice, voice, or sentence fluency. Conventions are important, but if we let ourselves or students focus on these surface features first, we can hinder the writer's idea generation and thinking ability. Writing is not spelling well or having perfect grammar. Writing is conveying your ideas effectively and engaging your audience. For these reasons, we waited until now to address grammar and conventions. We refer to conventions as "polishing," and we can't begin to polish until we have something meaningful to polish.

Our first instinct, as constructivist educators, is to avoid the type of grammar game we describe below, because we fear that it encourages out-of-context grammar drills. However, the goal is for the game to be a useful learning tool as students realize that conventions *must* be considered in the context of the writer's meaning. If this game goes according to plan, rich student dialogue will ensue about the meaning of particular conventions and the inherent connection to the author's intention.

Student Learning Objectives:

- Students articulate how the writer's intentions impact the use of punctuation and how punctuation affects the meaning of the text.
- Students play with language, punctuation, and spelling and explore their effects on meaning.

Common Core Standards Addressed:

ELA and Literacy, Writing Anchor Standard 4: Produce clear and coherent writing in which the development and organization are appropriate to the task, purpose, and audience.
ELA and Literacy, Writing Anchor Standard 5: With guidance and support from peers and adults, develop and strengthen writing as

needed by planning, revising, editing, rewriting, or trying a new approach.

Resources/Material:

- The "find the mistake" grammar game sentences taken from the writing sample titled "The Park" in Appendix A. The backslash marks (/) indicate the separate game sentences to display in random order on a white board, overhead projector, or interactive white board. (The teacher will have to type or write these for display.)
- The whole writing sample titled "The Park" to display for students on the board.
- Copy of the Conventions Question Chart for each student.

Overview of Lesson:

- The class plays a "find the mistake" type of grammar game to solicit discussion about the effects of punctuation on meaning.
- Students review one of their quickwrites and edit for grammar and conventions, considering the question "What did I mean here?"
- Students share their quickwrite with a partner and talk about the convention *options* in their pieces.

The Engagement:

- **Play the "find the mistake" grammar game:** Divide the students into two groups and have students take turns coming up to a desk that will serve as their "buzzer." Display the first sentence/example. Students hit the desk when their team finds a conventions or grammatical mistake in the sentence and states the mistake and correction for the class. The buzzer student may consult with his or her teammates, if necessary, but they only have 15 seconds to do so. If the team who buzzes in first does not have an answer within 15 seconds, the other team gets a chance to answer with the same procedures. Award one point for each correct answer. The team with the most points wins.
- **Encourage dialogue:** Students will begin to disagree with each other about the "correct" edit. This is when the lesson *really* begins. The discrepancy between suggested edits will open dialogue about how punctuation changes the meaning of a text and the way we read what is written. In order to facilitate such questioning, you can

interject questions such as *"What do you think the writer meant here?"* If students from both teams can identify a correction with a logical, grammatical rationale, both should earn a point for their team.

The following is an example of the disputes among our students:

Game Sentence: I like to go to the park, there were lots of things to do there.

Student Dialogue:

Ray: It should say, I like to go to the park, period. There were lots of things to do there.

Steve: No, can't it be, I like to go to the park. There are lots of things to do there.

Teacher: What's the difference between the two?

Ray: He **used** to like going to the park, maybe when he was a kid or something.

Steve: Oh, I didn't think about that. I thought that it was a kid writing it and that they meant to say "are" instead of "were."

Teacher: I think you're both right and make a good point. We don't know what the author meant. But, when you're the author, you'll know what you're trying to say.

- **Put it in context:** Once you have gone through all the game sentences, display the sample writing titled "The Park" (in Appendix A). All of the game sentences came from this sample writing. The sample provides a meaningful context for students to use in inferring the writer's meaning and may help answer some of the students' questions about the appropriate conventions for the game sentences. Use this opportunity to emphasize that grammar and conventions are tied to the writer's meaning.

Student Practice:

- After the game, direct students back to their **writer's notebook** to find a quickwrite of their choice, one that they like, to reread and edit. Tell students that this is their opportunity to use their understanding of punctuation to play with their sentences. Remind them that the goal is to make sure they convey their meaning clearly with the conventions that fit. Give students time to read and edit their quickwrite independently.
- Hand out and introduce the **Conventions Question Chart** to students. Read the questions aloud and discuss any ones that students are unsure of.

- Then, pair students up and ask them to **coach each other on their quickwrite**, with a focus on conventions. Set the rule that students are *not* to simply mark up edits on their partner's paper. They are to *talk* about the convention options and let the writer decide what he or she meant. Remind them to use the Conventions Question Chart for assistance if they get stuck during the editing conversations.
- Students could do a second reread for spelling corrections.
- **Explain** to students that this editing process is the same type of process they would do at the publishing stage when they wanted to polish a piece of writing to share with others. If you conduct writing workshop in your classroom, you could use these activities to help students learn to edit their work. Research has shown that teaching students to self-edit is an effective means of improving their written grammar (Lyman, 1931, quoted in Braddock et al., 1963).

Teacher Reflection:

Heather Corbett, one of the 5th-grade teachers at Skyline, felt some tension between her beliefs about good teaching and this conventions game when we first tried it out. This is her reflection on the lesson:

When the "convention game" was first introduced to my students, it was structured with students in teams and the sentences or paragraphs were projected on the board. The person who "buzzed" in first (by hitting the desk) was to correct the convention mistake in the writing. This was so different from anything I had done in my classroom—the competition, the race, hitting the desk—I didn't like it, but then something happened. The game was interrupted with this rich dialogue! The students disagreed on what the corrections should be. They wanted to know (as Paul Harvey would say) "the rest of the story." We began talking about how different punctuation would change the meaning; it wasn't as simple as just saying, "Add a comma here," or "it needs a period there." Rather, they were asking, "What was the author trying to say?" They wondered who the writer was speaking to. The students argued about how the sentences should be changed and became invested in defending their opinion of the "correct" answer. This was where the learning happened, and it was much deeper than any of us had expected. In the end, I realized that the game served as a mechanism to have students buy-in to learning about conventions, and it also livened up what could have been a dull subject of study. We never got through all the sentence slides, but the students had a fantastic discussion about the meaning of various grammar conventions.

Week 8: Practice Peer Tutoring

Length of the Lesson: One 45-minute session

Student Learning Objectives:

- Students synthesize their learning by employing the peer tutoring strategies they have learned over the last several weeks.
- Students summarize the strategies involved in being an effective writing tutor.

Common Core Standards Addressed:

ELA and Literacy, Writing Anchor Standard 5: With guidance and support from peers and adults, develop and strengthen writing as needed by planning, revising, editing, rewriting, or trying a new approach.

Resources/Material:

- Students' copies of each of the four Question Charts (some teachers copy these using a different color for each chart and spiral bind them for easy use)
- Students' copies of the WRITE Mnemonic Chart
- Each student will need a piece of writing to use to practice peer tutoring.

Overview of Lesson:

- Review the WRITE mnemonic to summarize the strategies involved in being a strong writing tutor.
- Students practice peer tutoring with classmates or with students from another class.

The Engagement:

- **Review principles of writing center pedagogy:** Explain to students that they will be tutoring a peer today and need to review what they want to do to be effective writing tutors. Ask students to summarize the tutoring strategies they have learned: *"What will you do to make your tutoring session successful? What are the steps and strategies a good writing tutor uses?"* If you use writer's notebooks, you can have students make a summary list in their notebooks. If not, you can make a list of the tutoring strategies on the board. (The WRITE mnemonic also serves as a written visual of these principles.) If needed, prompt the students by asking, *"What will you do first?"*

- **Review the WRITE mnemonic.** In their discussion of what makes a good writing tutor, students will ideally mention the following: Introduce yourself, be friendly, get to know the person a little (establish rapport), ask about the writing assignment, ask the writer to read the piece aloud, respect the writer and the writer's paper, focus on content/ideas/organization first, be a good listener, respond as a reader, ask open-ended questions, give the writer "wait time" to think, ask the writer what she or he is having trouble with, be positive and encouraging, and leave the writer with one or two specific suggestions.

Student Practice:

- Tell students to have their **WRITE Mnemonic Chart** and all **four Question Charts** handy for the tutoring practice session. Remind them that the Question Charts are there for support if they get stuck in their writing conversations but that they do not need to use those questions exactly or in any order. They can just let the conversation flow naturally.
- **Pair Up Students:** If possible, team up with another teacher in your grade level to pair up students so that tutors will be working with someone from outside their regular group. This will give students the opportunity to work with a new writer.
- Give students 10–12 minutes for the **first round of peer tutoring**. Students can select who would like to be the writer and who would like to be the tutor first. After the time is up, have students switch roles. Give the new tutors 10–12 minutes for the **second round of peer tutoring**.
- **Debrief:** After both rounds of peer tutoring are complete, bring the whole class together to debrief. Ask, *"What did your tutor do that you found helpful as a writer?"* or *"What questions did your tutor ask that helped you think differently about your writing?"* Also encourage students to discuss any challenges they faced: *"We need to be respectful of each other, but we also want to put our heads together to solve any difficulties we had. Was there anything that was difficult or challenging about the tutoring session?"*
- **The Writing Center:** Tell students when and where the writing center will be opening. Explain that anyone can volunteer to be a tutor in the writing center. Tell them which grade-level students will be coming to the writing center to work on their writing. Drum up excitement for the writing center, and praise students for all the work they've done!

CONCLUDING THOUGHTS ABOUT THE LESSON PLANS

Our peer tutoring unit of lessons serves as a strong foundation for student conversations about writing and for students' development of their own writing. However, one or two lessons on the stages of the writing process or the various traits of quality writing are not enough. It's a great start, but these concepts will have to be taught many times, in different ways, with different mentor texts and genres, in order for students to become more comfortable integrating these skills and strategies. Writers spend a lifetime developing the craft of voice or persuasion or just the right amount of detail. Check out Ralph Fletcher and Joann Portalupi's *Craft Lessons—K–8* and Joann Portalupi and Ralph Fletcher's *Nonfiction Craft Lessons*, Elizabeth Hale's *Crafting Writers K–6*, and Georgia Heard's *Revision Toolbox* for additional lessons on the traits of good writing and writing processes. These resources also have lesson ideas for primary grades.

These eight lessons are a great way to launch the year and begin writing with students. If you started the peer tutoring lessons right at the beginning of the year, you could have your writing center open for business by the beginning of November! It would also work well to begin the peer tutoring unit around October 1. Be careful, though: Since the second quarter is often filled with holiday activities, the days easily get packed with other things. You would want to finish the peer tutoring unit prior to winter break so that you can open your writing center in January or February, when school starts back up. Most teachers find that in January students need something new—new routines, new units of study, new desk arrangements, and so forth. Launching the writing center at this time could be just the new thing your students need, giving them something exciting to work toward and added responsibility to keep them engaged. Of course, you may need to do a little review, perhaps reteaching Lesson 8, after the break to get students back into the groove of tutoring and draw their tutoring knowledge back up to the forefront of their minds.

WRITE Mnemonic Chart

W
ATCH FOR THE IDEAS AND ORGANIZATION FIRST.

Set a plan for the session. Ask the writer about the assignment and his or her goals for the paper.

Pay attention to the most important things first, like the ideas and organization. Then look for words, sentences, or spelling that need to be changed.

R
ESPECT THE WRITER AND THE WRITER'S PAPER.

Be friendly and polite. Make the writer feel comfortable.

Don't write on the writer's paper! The writer gets to decide exactly what to write or change.

Be an active listener and show interest.

Sit next to the writer, and ask him or her to read the paper aloud.

I
NVOLVE THE WRITER BY ASKING QUESTIONS.

Writers learn more if they are allowed to answer questions about their papers.

Ask open-ended questions such as "What can I help you with?" or "What do you really want readers to know?"

Give "wait time" for the writer to respond.

T
EACH THE WRITER TO WRITE BETTER.

Give suggestions that will make the paper better and present strategies the writer can use (such as "show, don't tell").

Explain and give examples so the writer understands your suggestions.

Be helpful and friendly. Treat writers as you would want to be treated.

E
NCOURAGE THE STUDENT.

Compliment at least one or two things about a paper (not just the parts you worked on) to show the writer that he or she is doing well.

Use "I statements" to point out problems in the writing.

Respond as a reader, and share your natural, emotional responses to the piece.

Think of yourself as a coach, not a critic.

Adapted from Brad Wilcox "Conferencing Tips." *Writing Lab Newsletter* (April 1984). Reproduced with permission from NCTE.

Content and Ideas Question Chart

What was your assignment?
Will you read your paper aloud to me?

Questions to Ask Yourself	Questions to Ask the Writer
• Is the topic small enough or big enough for the assignment?	• What is your topic? • Could you tell me more about this? • How could you make your topic smaller? or bigger?
• Can you figure out the main idea of the paper or theme of the story?	• What is most important about _____?
• Does the paper **show** rather than **tell**?	• How could you **show** this idea rather than just **tell**ing us what you think? • Could you give me an example of this? • What else could you say about this?
• Do the details make the main idea stronger? Are there enough details?	• Does this part need to be in there? • How can you connect this information to the main idea? *Or—* How can you make sure readers understand your theme?
• **What can be improved on this paper?**	• How could you make that clearer? • What ideas do you want to talk through? • What part do you think needs work?

Organization Question Chart

What was your assignment?
Will you read your paper aloud to me?

Questions to Ask Yourself	Questions to Ask the Writer
• Is the main idea or message clear?	• What is the main idea or message you want readers to get from this writing? • How can you organize your ideas to highlight that main idea/message?
• Does the beginning catch my attention?	• How could you catch the reader's attention at the beginning?
• Can I follow the paper?	• I am having trouble following here. What could you add (or take out) to make it clearer?
• Do any parts need to be in a different order to make more sense?	• Can you retell the sequence of events to me? Do the events in your paper match what you said? • What if you moved [this] part to [this] place?
• Is there a part of the writing or detail that doesn't seem to fit with the rest of the paper?	• Can you tell me more about [this]? Why is it important to the story or topic?
• Is there an ending? Does the ending fit the pattern of the paper?	• How could you make your ending fit with the organization of your paper?

Word Choice and Sentence Fluency Question Chart

What was your assignment?
Will you read your paper aloud to me?

Questions to Ask Yourself	Questions to Ask the Writer
• Do the words paint a picture?	• What words could you use so that they paint a picture for the reader? • Is there a more specific noun or verb you can use here?
• Do the sentences make sense?	• I am having trouble understanding this part. How could you revise this sentence to make it clearer?
• Is the paper easy to read out loud?	• How could you reword your sentence to make it easier to read out loud or smoother?
• Are there a variety of sentence lengths and beginning phrases for sentences?	• I noticed a few of these sentences begin the same way. How could you reword one of them to make it begin differently?
• Are there several really short sentences?	• How can you combine some of these sentences so that they flow smoother?
• Are some sentences really long or run-on sentences?	• How can you break this sentence into two separate sentences to make it clearer?

Conventions Question Chart

Questions to Ask Yourself	Questions to Ask the Writer
• Are the correct words capitalized?	• I noticed you have a capital letter (or lowercase letter) here. Why did you put it there?
• Are all the words spelled correctly?	• I noticed this word is not spelled correctly. How else could you spell it? *Or*—Let's look it up in the dictionary.
• Is the punctuation (periods, question marks, commas, exclamation marks, and quotation marks) in the right place?	• Do you want this sentence to be a question, or a statement? Do you want to emphasize (!) your idea? • Did another person say this? If this is dialogue from a person, you can put in quotation marks to let readers know.
• Are apostrophes used properly?	• For this word, did you mean one thing, two things, or is it possessive?
• Are the verb tenses correct? Does the writing shift between past and present tenses?	• It seems like you're moving back and forth between past and present tenses. When did these events happen?
• Are paragraphs used to show where a new idea begins? Are the paragraphs indented properly?	• Which of these sentences introduces a new idea? Do you think that would be a good place to start a new paragraph, or is this part of the previous idea?

CHAPTER 7

The End of the Beginning

As we look across this work, we notice a few significant themes that speak to the power and purpose of elementary writing centers: (1) Peer tutoring serves as a democratizing agent and an empowering educational process for students; (2) peer tutoring is a site of productive social interaction and authentic social learning; and (3) writing centers employ a student-centered curriculum that places the teacher in the role of facilitator and learner and the students in the role of active thinker, autonomous learner, and collaborative partner. In this chapter, we discuss these themes and connect them to teachers' reflections on their writing center implementation.

PEER TUTORING AS A DEMOCRATIZING AND EMPOWERING PROCESS

Peer tutoring can be viewed as a democratizing process (Bomer & Bomer, 2001) because it involves rigorous, authentic instruction for all students and provides them with an opportunity to develop important leadership and interactional skills. Peer tutoring is guided by principles of equity and opportunity and therefore benefits tutors who struggle with school, writing, or social acceptance and respect. As educational theorist John Dewey (1916) noted, a democratic education should develop students' abilities to think about problems and their possible solutions. Peer tutoring enables struggling students to rise to the level of problem solver instead of accepting the label of "problem creator"—to rise to the level of thinker and contributor instead of continuing to be cast in the oppressive role of "poor student."

Carey Henderson was a 5th-grade teacher who saw Annie Ortiz's vision of empowered students come to fruition. In the beginning of this book, you read about how Annie predicted that her 5th-graders needed more responsibility to help harness their unchanneled energy. In this reflection, Carey sees Annie's prediction come alive:

Once I understood the concept of the writing center and was able to see the big picture, I was immediately excited and couldn't wait to get back to my room to tell my kids, *"You're* going to be the writing coaches!" Putting that responsibility and trust in them made them feel proud and big, and maybe even a little nervous. In the lessons that followed, I saw my students begin to really listen and participate with almost a sense of urgency, thinking, "I have to know what I'm doing!" They became invested in the project and idea and began to enjoy learning how to be a writing coach. Not only did the training teach them to be great evaluators of others' writing, it helped them become better writers as well. As the writing center opened and my 5th-graders began coaching 4th-graders, I was surprised at the number of students who wanted to coach. Not only was I shocked at the popularity but also with the students who volunteered to tutor. It wasn't my strongest readers and writers who wanted to go week after week.

You may recall early on when we stated that the best tutors weren't always the strongest students or the strongest writers. Often, the students who were rarely given leadership opportunities were the ones who were most eager to tutor and most committed to the work. Carey saw this phenomenon happening among her students. We reiterate the importance of opening the writing center up for all students who have received the training to tutor and for any writer in the selected grades to visit because this is how the equalizing potential of peer tutoring becomes realized.

The democratizing power of peer tutoring also lies in the development of students' critical literacy habits. If we truly want students to be able to move out of situations of poverty and oppression, we must teach them critical literacy skills that will enable them to consider and highlight multiple perspectives; "collaborate, deliberate and differ"; gather information through nonconfrontational and open-ended questioning methods; inquire; demonstrate respect for others as human beings and individuals; and engage in collaborative leadership rather than contribute to hierarchical power structures (Bomer & Bomer, 2001, p. 14). A logical extension of the lessons in this book would be lessons on critical literacy that explicitly name and describe these skills for students. If we teach students these thinking processes and give them the metalanguage to identify and understand what they are doing and why they are doing it, they will be able to transfer these skills to other learning engagements and other life activities. For example, a teacher could extend one of the peer tutoring lessons, after the writing center is up and running, with a follow-up lesson on considering and highlighting multiple perspectives. This lesson could be framed as an informational writing lesson in which students were encouraged to find multiple perspectives on a topic or issue they cared about and put these ideas in conversation with each other in their writing. Then, the teacher could connect this skill to tutoring and real-world interactions in which students would be essentially doing the same thing: considering multiple perspectives and figuring out how to engage in integrative rather than polarizing thinking.

PEER TUTORING AS POWERFUL SOCIAL INTERACTION

Peer tutoring can be a site of powerful social interaction and social learning. Social constructionist theory posits that knowledge is created in interaction and collaboration with others (Berger & Luckmann, 1967). Nothing is learned or known in a vacuum, void of influence from other human beings. Even an individual's observations of the natural world are shaped by the culture and language within which that person was brought up, and those concepts and meanings color the person's observations and perceptions of the world. As teachers, we often forget about the need for learning to be social and collaborative, and we think we are the ones imparting knowledge to the students or that the students are to gain information independently from a text. But learning is actually more complex and social than these methods allow. Peer tutoring provides an authentic and engaging social learning environment for students. Writers have a peer audience (one other than the teacher) and are able to engage in collaborative knowledge creation with their peer tutors.

Students' work in the writing center also serves as the collaborative practice phase in the Gradual Release of Responsibility model of instruction (Pearson & Gallagher, 1983). In the Gradual Release Model, there are five phases of learning or instruction: modeling, guided practice, collaborative practice, independent practice, and application in a new setting (transfer). With the tutor training lessons, the teacher models traits of good writing and provides students with the opportunity to try those elements out in their own writing, often through guided practice. The writing center then serves as an essential point of collaborative practice "for students to use the vocabulary and writing process and genre language that have been modeled by the teacher" (Englert et al., 1992, p. 415). This collaborative practice allows students to begin to internalize their knowledge about writing so that they can apply these strategies and skills independently in future writing contexts.

Jan Anderson was a 4th-grade teacher at Skyline Elementary who urged all her students to use their writing center. Below is her reflection on the social impact the tutoring sessions had on one of her writers.

> Jack was a student who typically struggled with learning in general and struggled with literacy quite a bit. When I told him to sign up for the writing center, he said he had nothing. I told him to go in with his writer's notebook and see what they could do for him. After visiting the writing center the first time, he came back all smiles and said he didn't get a piece written, but he had lots of great ideas. He immediately sat in the writing resource corner and began to write. He kept his head buried in his writing for 20 minutes, until I had to stop him to move on to another lesson.
>
> In my classroom, there is a corner full of resources to help with writing. I began to notice Jack spending a great deal of time there. He was not a student who I was used to seeing in the writing corner. He often struggled to get thoughts on paper. I thought it was great that he was using these resources, but I thought nothing more of it. Then I was discussing the writing center with my colleagues and learned that using the resources was a suggestion given to Jack from one of his writing tutors in the writing center!

Jack may have felt comforted by the writing resources (a dictionary, thesaurus, mentor texts, anchor charts, computer for Internet research), or he may have been encouraged by the idea that even proficient writers (like his writing tutor) need support in the writing process. The resources themselves may not have been the important factor; rather, it was most likely the confidence and support of a peer that gave Jack the confidence to try writing. Gersten and Baker (2001) studied struggling writers and found that peer collaboration was associated with strong positive writing outcomes and provided students with valuable feedback to improve their writing. Through peer support, writing centers help build the confidence of resistant writers and develop the writing skills of struggling writers (Gersten & Baker, 2001).

SHIFTING THE ROLE OF THE TEACHER

Writing centers employ a student-centered curriculum that shifts the roles of students and teachers. In the writing center, the teacher steps back and allows the students to take the lead and the initiative in their own knowledge creation. The role of the teacher shifts from that of authority and knowledge-provider to one of teacher-as-facilitator and teacher-as-learner. In the reflection below, we see a teacher taking the stance of a learner. John Hansen was a university writing tutor who was helping the Skyline Elementary students with their first writing center. He served as a writing center facilitator and supervisor, assisting students when they got stuck. John also taught freshman composition at OSU, and in this reflection, he is imagining the possibilities for this peer tutoring model with his college students.

> After Kyra (tutee) had read through her story about buying a puppy and her mother's reaction to her purchase, Brooke (tutor) first recognized that there needed to be designated quotation marks around each character's dialogue. Kyra seemed nauseated at the sight of this and a disgruntled expression crossed her face. Kyra was befuddled. As a result, Brooke centered the paper between them and pointed with her pencil to an example, which she read aloud to Kyra—in a warm and respectful manner. Much like a conductor of an orchestra would lead the symphony through difficult music frames with a baton, Brooke instructed Kyra through many of the errors with that pencil and helped lead her through the intricate writing process. A connection began to take place before my eyes.
>
> Another key concept that Brooke focused on was clarity. Clarity is an issue for writers at any grade level. Brooke posed these questions and suggestions to help Kyra comprehend the point about clarity: "How can you help the reader understand? Some of these sentences are too long and the ideas blend in with one another. This makes it hard to understand. How can you fix this?" Similarly, I have witnessed many students at the college level grapple with such matters in their writing. The statements by Brooke—her peer tutoring methods—were a prime example

of what I wanted to take place with my students in my own composition classes.

This reflection demonstrates a couple of important ideas: (1) This peer tutoring approach has value at any level of education, and (2) the teachers learn and benefit as much from the peer tutoring lessons and writing center supervision as the students. When teachers watch the tutoring sessions take place, we learn about our students, we learn about them as writers, and we learn how to talk about writing and support a writer's growth. As Donald Graves (2003) says, if we watch them closely enough, our students will teach us how to teach them. The writing center puts students in the role of teacher and leader, it shifts the teacher to the roles of learner and facilitator, and it puts writers in control of their own writing development and improvement.

However, it is important that teachers step back without stepping *out*: They need to remain connected to the work of the writing center by regularly supervising and observing tutors and writers during their sessions. It is also important that writing center pedagogy is not seen as a laissez-faire or hands-off approach to teaching and learning; there is a great deal of explicit instruction before and after the tutoring sessions. Cate Pogue was a 5th-grade teacher whose students were trained to be peer tutors for Skyline's first writing center. Since their writing center was housed in the library, Cate didn't have the chance to see the writing center sessions in action. One day, she noticed a spontaneous tutoring session in progress when she was in the library and was curious to see how the students handled it.

I happened upon an impromptu, unofficial "tutoring session" in progress. I was in the library working at the computers with my 5th-grade class. Two 4th-graders were on two computers, side by side, and a third student was positioned between them. As I was walking around helping my students, I lingered behind the 4th-graders to see what they were working on. The two boys sitting at the computers were working on a poetry assignment, while the third was taking on the coaching role, on his own accord. He took his role seriously. He was the expert and kept the two boys focused. He asked questions: "Who are you writing to? Who is your audience—your mom? What does she like? What do you want to say to her?" He moved back and forth between the two writers. He was confident and proud and truly trying to help. You could almost see his wheels turning, thinking about what to ask to help prod them along. The boys looked to him for direction yet stayed true to their thoughts, ideas, and words. They focused on their moms—the audience. It was really incredible to see the process in action. These students were part of the tutoring experience so much (as writers who used the writing center) that they were taking on the mentor role without being prompted. It's becoming a natural response to help other writers in need. What the 5th-graders are modeling while tutoring helps the students in the moment, with that piece, but also helps the students go back and be able to have similar dialogue with their classmates.

Here, Cate is noticing an effect that we hadn't previously considered: Engaging in the peer tutoring process was helping the *writers* learn to be tutors in their own classrooms, with other peers. What an exciting trickle-down effect! The writers were acquiring the language of peer tutoring through the process of interacting with their writing tutors.

Returning to our main point about teachers being involved as facilitators in the writing center: Until Cate watched the writing center sessions herself, she really didn't understand the learning that was taking place and the dialogic process in which the students engaged. It is vital that all participating teachers and administrators have the opportunity to watch students at work in the writing center so that they understand what the students are doing and the magic of the social interaction and learning that takes place.

FINAL THOUGHTS

The End of the Beginning is a delightful novel by Avi for young readers about a snail and an ant who set off on a journey on a little branch of their tree. When they reach the end of their adventure, they realize that it's all just beginning. The same can be said for this book and your writing center. You are ready to begin your writing center adventure. This is just the beginning of a student-centered, socially engaging, process-based writing curriculum. You will certainly need to continue exploring other powerful writing practices to expand your pedagogy. We hope your journey is invigorating for you and your students, and that it is full of wondrous learning.

Supporting Materials for Tutoring Lessons

SUPPORTING MATERIALS FOR LESSON 1

Script for Using Play-Doh to Teach the Writing Process

by Rosemary Faucette

Reprinted from *Ideas Plus Book 15* (Faucette, 1997).
Used by permission of NCTE.

Today's lesson requires no pencil or paper, only your hands. While you work with your hands, please listen to me. It is important that you connect what you are doing with what I am saying.

From this activity today, you will be able to answer these questions: What process does a writer go through to produce a final piece? How is a writer like a sculptor? [I write these questions on the board to help students focus.]

To get ready, clear your desks and take out your Play-Doh and a pencil.

Close your eyes and get the feel of the clay in your hands. *Slowly* knead the dough. A writer must know the material before using it in a final piece. That's why it is important for you to read a variety of books and explore the dictionary and the thesaurus. These are places you find the material of writers.

What is the material of writers? Words! It is important that you play with words, experiment with words in journals or learning logs or letters or notes. A writer plays with words like a sculptor kneads clay. Take a few minutes now and play. See what this material can do. Stretch it. Pile it. Press it. Fold it. Don't make anything out of it. Just play. [I continue speaking while students do this.]

In a minute I am going to ask you to design something, but before I do, I want to introduce you to two parts of yourself that you may not know about. A writer, like a sculptor, has two parts that work together to produce a final piece. These two parts are what we call the *creator* and the *critic*. Which do you think has a bigger part in the first stages of writing or sculpting? It's the creator, the uncensored part, the part of you that envisions ideas, brainstorms possibilities, and conceives of all sorts of ways to do something.

When do you suppose the critic starts to work? Your critic part jumps up when you need to decide, when you need to analyze, revise, or edit, when a judgment call is needed. If you hear a voice starting to make judgments when you are still in the prewriting stages, when you are still just getting ideas for your writing, tell that voice to be quiet and wait for its turn.

Today you will create something. You will put it on display for other students and their parents to see. So your audience is more than just you or me. Your audience is all the other students and parents. It is important to know who your audience is before you begin, because knowing your audience can affect what you create.

You cannot begin until you know what your purpose is, just as a writer cannot begin to write until she knows what her purpose is, why she is writing. Today your purpose is to create a pencil holder—something that will hold a pencil on your desk. A purpose focuses our intentions. It sets a path, a destination.

I want you to start to create the first of many ideas you will come up with for a pencil holder. Don't decide on the final product yet. Just experiment with lots of ideas. Listen while you work.

A writer always has a purpose. It may be to describe something, or to explain something, or to tell a story. Sometimes the purpose may just be to get rid of anger or sadness—just to put things down on paper that the writer can't say aloud. Sometimes a writer may write to persuade. Other times a writer's purpose might be to give information, such as explaining to someone how to print a document on the computer or how to get from your house to school. A writer may write to explore how he feels about something. His purpose may be to find out what he thinks.

Okay, mush up your dough, and start again. I know you don't like destroying your first creation, but I want to prove to you that there are thousands more ideas where that one came from. What part of you came up with that first design? That's right, your creator, and your creator is anxious to give you more ideas. Start another design. As you do, please listen. The creative process has many stages. As a sculptor, the one you are experiencing right now might be called *presculpting*. In writing, it is called *prewriting* or *rehearsing*. It is the time when you are getting ideas and putting them together in new ways, preparing for the final production. During this stage only your creator is at work. Your critic is asleep. For some of you, your critic wants to come out and judge, judge, judge. Tell your critic politely to be quiet. As you rehearse, keep your purpose in mind. Ask yourself: "What am I trying to accomplish? How do I want my audience to feel?" This will keep you focused . . . Take a couple of minutes to try something new and different from your last design. [I allow students a couple of minutes to start again.]

Okay, now mush it up. Let's start again. But before you do, let's discuss what it is you want to achieve in this piece, because we are getting ready to do a first draft. What criteria shall we use to judge this piece? [At this point we spend a few minutes talking about how we want to judge the pieces. My students' comments always lead eventually to the ideas of beauty (aesthetics; sensory appeal; is it pleasing to look at or touch?), function (usefulness; practicality; does it do what it was intended to?), and creativity (originality; imaginativeness; does it surprise or amuse you?). I write the criteria we come up with on the board.]

Keep these criteria in mind as you design. This time will be your last. Let your critic help you pick out your best idea or combine your ideas to create an entirely new pencil holder. This last design will be your first draft of your final piece. You have 5 minutes. Please work in silence. [I let students know when there is 1 minute remaining in the work time.]

You have finished your first draft. A writer, like a sculptor, thinks about how the audience will respond to his or her work. The writer, like the sculptor, may stop at any point and get responses from other people. Ask your partner to look at your design and tell you if he or she knows where the pencil will go. This will show that you have given your form meaning. It is not just a lot of Play-Doh thrown together—it has one idea or purpose. This quality is often called *unity*. This one idea should be obvious to your response partner. If not, you haven't focused your ideas clearly enough.

You have now gone through two stages of the writing process: (1) rehearsals to come up with lots of ideas and (2) a first draft to get the essential meaning. Now let's move on to the revision stage.

Revision literally means "to see again." So I want you to look at your pencil holder from various points of view. This will help you see it in a new way. Then you can decide what you want to do to it. So stand on your chair or look at it from a distance. What do you see that you would like to change or refine? Now get in front of your desk and stoop down close. What do you want to change or refine? Now look at it from the side. Now from the other side. Now sit down.

You have looked at what needs to be refined. There will never be a time in your writing when you can't revise—even up to the end. Some people are still revising while they edit or while typing their final draft. That's because every time we reread our writing or "re-view" our pencil holders, we will "re-see" it and come up with a better way of saying or designing it.

One of the ways you can revise is to do what you just did—look at your work from another point of view or have someone else read it and comment. So right now, let your partner look at it, and then listen to his or her ideas for improving it. You don't have to take your partner's suggestions, but think about them, and make any revisions that you think will improve your pencil holder. [Students confer and revise briefly.]

Now you are ready to begin the final stage—editing. At this point a writer looks closely at details such as spelling, punctuation, and capitalization, which help make the writing clear and readable. Since this is detail work, trade a little colored Play-Doh with your partner or someone nearby so that you can add any necessary finishing touches to your pencil holder. [I allow a few minutes here.]

The details you just added are only finishing touches. You could have a lot of nice little details on your pencil holder, but if it doesn't have meaning, if it doesn't have unity and hold together, these finishing touches aren't worth anything. The same is true for writing. Good spelling, punctuation, and usage are only important if the piece itself has meaning, unity, and coherence.

Now admire your product. A writer is like a sculptor. A writer, like a sculptor, like you today, goes through a process involving many changes that leads to a final product.

Give your final product a name. Write the name on a 3" x 5" card, set your pencil holder on the card, and display your sculpture. A writer is like a sculptor, sharing his or her work with the public. Put your final product on display so all can see.

Let's walk around the room quietly looking at each masterpiece. Please keep comments to yourself right now. [We review the final products.]

Now it is time for comments: Look at your partner's piece. Pick one positive comment you would like to use to admire the piece aloud. Stand up and tell the class. And let's applaud each sculptor/writer.

EXTENSIONS ON THE METAPHORICAL INTRODUCTION TO THE WRITING PROCESS

By Annie Ortiz

The Paper Airplane: For 2nd-Graders

The 5th grade used clay as a metaphorical introduction to the writing process. I wondered how I could replicate this metaphor for each grade level without stealing 5th grade's thunder. I searched for metaphors for writing and found some I thought I could build upon.

In 2nd grade, the metaphor was paper airplanes. I tried to simplify the writing process into steps that were familiar to 2nd-graders: *first, next, then,* and *last*. In my head, *first* would be imagining the book, brainstorming of possibilities. *Next* would be the writing or drafting stage, and *then* would encompass revising and editing processes. *Last* would be the publishing or enjoying the finished book. This was a simplified version of the writing process but one I thought younger children could relate to and identify later.

Armed with a stack of scrap paper, I entered a 2nd-grade classroom filled with eager children. After I told them we were going to make paper airplanes, the room erupted with "Oohs" and "Yes!" I told them to think about how making a paper airplane was like writing a book, because we would come back to that idea.

We gathered in a circle on the floor and proceeded with the process of making a paper airplane in *complete silence*. I held up my paper and folded it in half and then showed them. I continued step by step as they mimicked my folds. If someone was stuck, I scooted over to them and helped. When all airplanes were made, they chose a marker from a tub and wrote their name and a decoration on the side of the plane, still in silence.

One small group at a time lined up on one side of the room and launched their planes. The rest of us counted down and enjoyed the various flights. The class then had a chance to refold or fix any part of their planes and launched them again. We enjoyed a second set of airplanes swishing through the air. As one group stashed their planes in their cubbies, another group got ready for launch. We continued until everyone shared, and then settled back on the floor to talk about how making a paper airplane was like writing a book.

I asked what we did *first*. They responded with "Folded it," "Took the papers," or "Made a triangle." I asked, "Before we ever folded it, what did you do?" They said, "Got excited." I told them their excitement was because they had imagined the paper airplane before we ever made it. They got a picture in their head of the cool planes they could make. I then explained how that's exactly what writers do: They imagine the type of thing they might write. I showed them a variety of examples:

- *Dirt on My Shirt* by Jeff Foxworthy: He must have imagined writing poems about his family and growing up.
- *What's This?* by Judith McKinnon: She must have wondered about how little things looked up close. She also wrote six things about each item.
- *In the Swim* by Douglas Florian: He imagined a book of poems about things that swim.
- *True or False Rocks and Minerals* by Melvin and Gilda Berger: I told them these authors have the same last name. Maybe they were brother and sister or husband and wife. Writers can work together to write books. They must have wanted a guessing type book that also gave information about rocks.
- *How to Lose Your Friends* by Nancy Carlson: She told about a serious subject—treating friends nicely—in a very funny way.
- *ABC Alphab'art* by Anne Guery and Olivier Dussutour: Again I explained how writers work together. These authors imagined an ABC book, but with great works of art, where readers had to find the letter of the alphabet in each image.

I asked what we did *next*. They said, "Made it" (the paper airplane), and the students were able to identify exactly what writers would do at this stage: write. *Then* I asked about our next step. They knew they tried out the plane and had a chance to fix it and try it again. They also knew writers would share their writing with other writers. I told them that sometimes writers even went back and found better words or added details just like we did with the markers. We added details on our planes. Sometimes writers fixed words or punctuation marks so it would make their writing easy for another reader to enjoy.

We discussed the last step in our airplane-making process: *Last* we flew the planes, enjoying the countdown and the planes landing all over the room. I held one of the books I had used as a sample earlier and asked how the author might have felt when he or she finally had a book to share with others. The students knew the authors were very excited—just like the students were with their planes. I left the room feeling that this young group of writers knew the process we were about to embark upon. They could imagine a story, write it, revise it, and share it with others.

The Puzzle: For 3rd-Graders

Excited about the writing process narrowed down into manageable chunks for young children, I searched for a metaphor for 3rd-grade students. I came upon the idea of puzzles. I headed to our local dollar store and found four puzzles that had 24 or 25 pieces—puzzles that could be completed quickly. I took five or six pieces out of each puzzle and distributed the pieces among the other 3 boxes. Each puzzle now held most of the original pieces and pieces from the other 3 puzzles.

When I went into the 3rd-grade classrooms, I told the students that they were going to put together some puzzles and showed them the puzzle boxes with the pictures. They "Oohed" and "Yessed" at the superheroes and cute little bears. Before they completed the puzzles, I asked them to think about how putting together a puzzle was like writing a book. I followed the same steps to describe the creative process: *first, next, then,* and *last.* I wrote these steps on the board ("first," "next," "then," and "last") to remind students to think about these steps in the creative process as they built their puzzles.

They headed to their tables and began by dumping out all the pieces. Some started with the corners and others looked for random pieces. Near the end, they noticed the pieces didn't fit or they didn't have what they needed. They began to check around with other tables because they had seen the four puzzles at the beginning of the lesson. When all puzzles were complete, we gathered together on the floor.

I asked them what they did *first.* Some students said they "grabbed pieces," while others explained how they began with the corner pieces. I asked what they did before that. They remembered they looked at the picture on the box. They saw the finished puzzle. I told them that's what authors do—see or imagine what their finished piece might be and who might read it. Then I showed them a stack of published books, as I had done for the 2nd-graders, and explained how those authors might have imagined their final products.

The students were able to describe the *next* stage in a flash. They talked about how they put together the puzzle, and I helped them connect this process to how an author would put together the ideas of a book or piece of writing. To explain the third stage, the *then* portion, I asked students what they had to do before they could enjoy the finished puzzle. They remembered they had to go search out pieces from other tables or give pieces to other tables. As we discussed this process, they were able to compare it to how writers get ideas from other writers. I described how they had to fix their puzzle a little with help from others and made the connection to how a writer gets help with a piece of writing by going to friends for suggestions. Writing friends might help a writer change words, find missing parts, consider details to add, or help edit for spelling or punctuation. *Last* we enjoyed the finished puzzles and felt a sense of satisfaction as a result of figuring them out; students compared this step to a finished book or finished piece of writing. Readers get to enjoy the book like we enjoyed the puzzles.

Another grade level had a tangible way to think about the writing process. They too could imagine a story, write it, revise it, and share it with others when it was published.

The Gardener: For 4th-Graders

The metaphor strategy was working with 2nd- and 3rd-graders, so I was challenged to find one that might work with 4th-graders. I knew that one of their science kits the previous year was *Plant Growth and Development*. I thought gardening was a natural metaphor to use for the writing process. I purchased pots, soil, flowers, bulbs, fertilizer, and a cheap drop cloth.

Narrowing down the writing process to the steps of *first, next, then,* and *last* was working, so I decided not to change this format. I headed into a 4th-grade classroom, spread out the drop cloth, and set out all the materials. As the class gathered around the drop cloth, I asked them to imagine what the pots filled with flowers might look like in a few weeks or months. I told them as we planted the pots to think about how planting a garden is like the writing process.

In small groups, they added soil, sprinkled in fertilizer, placed the bulbs, added flowers, and topped off the pot with more soil. They looked satisfied as they brushed off the last bits of soil and sprinkled the plants with water. We set the pots aside and began to compare planting a garden with the writing process.

First, they pictured the pots filled with pansies throughout the winter. They knew this was what an author does—gets an idea in his or her head. I showed them examples of books authors imagined and the audiences they might have targeted as readers. *Next*, they identified the planting stage as the writing an author did. Authors got to work and wrote their first drafts. *Then*, we discussed revision and editing: all the additional steps an author and a planter might take to make the product turn out the way they want it to look. Students listed things they did while planting and compared those actions to the writing process. They added fertilizer like an author might add details. They planted bulbs that would come out later, just like an author might leave surprises at the end of a chapter to keep a reader interested. They also pruned "dead heads" or yellowing leaves like an author prunes words or parts he or she doesn't want in the story. Students brushed the soil off the edges of the pot like an author polishes off words or fixes punctuation. *Last,* they enjoyed the potted plants just as they imagined the elderly ladies, to whom they would be donating the plants, doing. They knew that this sharing process was like an author setting out his or her books to be enjoyed by readers.

SUPPORTING MATERIALS FOR LESSON 6

Word Choice and Sentence Fluency—Writing Sample

The Park

I like to go to the park. It is fun. There are lots of fun things to do at the park. I play with my baby brother. We run and we play. There are ducks at the pond there. The ducks are fun to watch. They swim on the water. You can feed the ducks. Ducks are fun to watch. There are sports things to do at the park. There are also picnic benches at the park. At the picnic benches sometimes people bring their lunch and they eat at the picnic benches and have parties there too with lots of balloons and tablecloths. People shoot fireworks there. They do this on the Fourth of July. People decorate the park at Christmas. They put up lots of lights.

SUPPORTING MATERIALS FOR LESSON 7

Grammar Game Writing Sample

The Park

I like to go to the Park, there were lots of things to do at the Park, you can feed the ducks, have a picnic at the Picnic Benches, or play Basket Ball or Tennis. / Some Times people shoot Fireworks there on the Forth of July. / People will decorated the park at Christmas. / They put up lots of lites. / Elfs and Santa gave away candy. / There were Monkey Bars Sweings, a tall slide, and a Merry-Go-Round. / There is also a sand box. Sometimes my friend and I like to see who swung the highest. / My little brother Jake liked to go also. / He like to feed the ducks. / On most days there is always something new to do or see, which made going to the Park lots of fun for everybody.

Student Writing Samples for Tutoring Practice

SAMPLE 3RD-GRADE STUDENT WRITING

Gracie and the Kitten

On March 19th my birthday my mom was making me a special breakfast. "Huh, mom? What's that sound?" "Rawww . . . ." I looked out my bedroom window. "Hey mom! Look I found a kitten!" I went to the kitchen to get tuna and gave it to him. I opened my window and let him in. He was so cute. He ate slowly. I went to show my mom, dad, and 9 year old brother Dillon. I left the kitten alone in my room and he walked out the window. I went to give him a ball of yarn but I couldn't find him. So I looked everywhere except under my bed. Then I checked under the bed and I FOUND HIM! The End.

SAMPLE 4TH-GRADE STUDENT WRITING

Shrews

Do you no a mammle that lives in a burrow in the warm dirt? Well a shrew does! In the shrews burrow the shrew bilds paths that split in two like a road. The shrew are vary good diggers so are earthworms. They use there nose, paws, and claws to dig in the dirt. But how do they use their nose to dig? Shrews have long, poynty noses that can break a part the soil so they can make there warm homes. A shrew gives birth to little pink baby shrews in her nest that she bilt down a secret little path in her burrow.

SAMPLE 5TH-GRADE STUDENT WRITING

Saving the Snow Leopards

A long time ago, Aztec solgers killed snow leopard. Thay wonted their fur and thay thought it gave them the power of the snow leopard. Then snow leopards became extinct in Mexico. Since the snow leopard became extinct Aztec solgers had no pretecshun agenst the winter snow.

Snow leopards live in Asia and some of Rusha. They're endangered to do poachers. Another reason snow leopards are endangered is because of its food sorse. Their food sorse level is terrible. Since there is no food, that makes them go to nearby villages.

The snow leopard depends on it's camouflage. But globle warming is melting the snow off the rocks. That makes them be spotted by its prey.

The snow leopard's diet is chickens, goat, antelope, and pronghorn. But it's main diet is chickens, goat, and pronghorn. Its enemies are snakes, hunters, and human. We get mad at snow leopards because we think they eat our chickens. But the pythons eat the chickens. But the snow leopard gets blamed. So we shoot the snow leopard.

In the summer snow leopards go up the mountin, in the winter snow leopards go down the mountin. There is a way you can help. Stop globle warming. Stop poaching. There is some snow leopards in captivity. The government wonts to save the snow leopard species. There numbers are stedily growing.

References

Anderson, J. (2005). *Mechanically inclined: Building grammar, usage, and style into writer's workshop.* Portland, ME: Stenhouse.

Bakhtin, M. M. (1986). *Speech genres and other late essays.* Austin, TX: University of Texas Press.

Bamford, R., & Kristo, J. (Eds.). (1998). *Making facts come alive: Choosing quality nonfiction literature K–8.* Norwood, MA: Christopher Gordon.

Bear, D., Invernizzi, M. A., Templeton, S., & Johnston, F. A. (2013). *Words their way: Word study for phonics, vocabulary, and spelling instruction* (5th ed.). Boston, MA: Pearson.

Berger, P. L., & Luckmann, T. (1967). *The social construction of reality: A treatise in the sociology of knowledge.* New York, NY: Anchor Books, Random House.

Berlin, J. A. (2003). Contemporary composition: The major pedagogical theories. In V. Villanueva (Ed.) *Cross-talk in comp theory* (pp. 255–270). Urbana, IL: National Council of Teachers of English. (Original work published 1982)

Bomer, R., & Bomer, K. (2001). *For a better world: Reading and writing for social action.* Portsmouth, NH: Heinemann.

Bond, V., & Simon, T. R. (2011). *Zora and me.* Somerville, MA: Candlewick.

Boquet, E. H. (1999). "Our Little Secret": A history of writing centers, pre- to post-open admissions. *College Composition and Communication, 50*(3), 463–482.

Braddock, R., Lloyd-Jones, R., & Schoer, L. (1963). *Research in written composition.* Urbana, IL: NCTE.

Britton, J., Burgess, T., & Martin, N. (1975). *The development of writing abilities (11–18).* London, England: Macmillan Education.

Britton, J., Burgess, T., Martin, N., McLeod, A., & Rosen, H. (2009). Shaping at the point of utterance. In S. Miller (Ed.), *The Norton book of composition studies* (pp. 461–466). New York, NY: W. W. Norton. (Original work published 1980).

Bruffee, K. (1984). Collaborative learning and the "Conversation of Mankind." *College English, 46*(7), 635–652.

Byers, G. O. (2001). *Daily oral language: 180 lessons and 18 assessments.* Greensboro, NC: Carson-Dellosa.

Calfee, R. C., & Miller, R. G. (2013). Best practices in writing assessment and instruction. In S. Graham, C. A. MacArthur, & J. Fitzgerald (Eds.), *Best practices in writing instruction* (2nd ed., pp. 351–377). New York, NY: The Guildford Press.

Calkins, L. (1980). When children want to punctuate: Basic skills belong in context. *Language Arts, 57*(5), 567–573.

Calkins, L. (1983). *Lessons from a child: On the teaching and learning of writing.* Portsmouth, NH: Heinemann Educational Books.

Calkins, L. (1994). *The Art of Teaching Writing.* Portsmouth, NH: Heinemann.

Carino, P. (1995). Early writing centers: Toward a history. *The Writing Center Journal, 15*(2), 103–115.

Chapman, M. (2006). Preschool through elementary writing. In P. Smagorinsky (Ed.), *Research on composition: Multiple perspectives on two decades of change* (pp. 15–47). New York, NY: Teachers College Press.

Cooper. E. (2010). *Farm.* New York, NY: Orchard Books .

Crotty, M. (1998). *The foundations of social research: Meaning and perspective in the research process.* Thousand Oaks, CA: SAGE.

Dean-Rumsey, T. A. (1998). Improving the writing skills of at-risk students through the use of writing across the curriculum and writing process instruction. *Dissertation Abstracts International, 37*(06A), 1598. (UMI No. AAI1395724).

DeCristofano, C. C. (2012). *A black hole is not a hole.* Watertown, MA: Charlesbridge.

DeVitt, A. (2008). *Writing genres.* Carbondale, IL: Southern Illinois University Press.

Dewey, J. (1916). *Democracy and education.* New York, NY: The Free Press.

Dewey, J. (1934). *Art as experience.* New York, NY: Penguin Group.

Duke, N. (2013, September). *Increasing engagement with informational text in the age of CCSS.* Presentation at Oklahoma Reading Association fall conference, Oklahoma City, OK.

Duke, N., Caughlin, S., Juzwik, M., & Martin, N. (2011). *Reading and writing genre with purpose in K–8 classrooms.* Portsmouth, NH: Heinemann.

Duke, N., & Pearson, D. (2002). Effective practices for developing reading comprehension. In A. Farstrup & S. J. Samuels (Eds.), *What research has to say about reading instruction* (pp. 205–242). Newark, DE: International Reading Association.

Duke, N., & Purcell-Gates, V. (2003). Genres at home and at school: Bridging the known to the new. *The Reading Teacher, 57*(1), 30–37.

Dyson, A. H. (1993). *Social worlds of children learning to write in an urban primary school.* New York, NY: Teachers College Press.

Ede, L., & Lunsford, A. (1984). Audience addressed/audience invoked: The role of audience in composition theory and pedagogy. In V. Villanueva (Ed.), *Cross-talk in comp theory* (2nd ed., pp. 77–95). Urbana, IL: National Council of Teachers of English.

Eisner, E. W. (2002). *Arts and the creation of mind.* New Haven, CN: Yale University Press.

Elbow, P. (1973). *Writing without teachers*. Oxford, UK: Oxford University Press.

Elbow, P. (2000). *Everyone can write*. New York, NY: Oxford University Press.

Emig, J. (1971). *The composing processes of twelfth graders*. Urbana, IL: National Council of Teachers of English.

Englert, C. S., Raphael, T. E., & Anderson, L. M. (1992). Socially mediated instruction: Improving students" knowledge and talk about writing. *The Elementary School Journal, 92*(4), 411–449.

Englert, C. S., Raphael, T. E., Anderson, L. M., Anthony, H. M., Stevens, D. D., & Fear, K. (1991). Making strategies and self-talk visible: Writing instruction in regular and special education classrooms. *American Educational Research Journal, 28*(2), 337–372.

Fang, Z. (2005). Scientific literacy: A systemic functional linguistics perspective. *Science Education, 89*(2), 335–347.

Faucette, R. (1997). Script for using Play-Doh to teach the writing process. In NCTE (Ed.), *Ideas plus: A collection of practical teaching ideas, Book 15*. Urbana, IL: NCTE.

Fels, D., & Wells, J. (2011). *The successful writing center: Building the best program with your students*. New York, NY: Teachers College Press.

Fitzgerald, L., & Ianetta, M. (2016). *The Oxford guide for writing tutors*. Oxford, England: Oxford University Press.

Fletcher, R. (1996). *A writer's notebook: Unlocking the writer within you*. New York, NY: Avon Books.

Fletcher, R., & Portalupi, J. (2007). *Craft lessons, K–8*. Portland, ME: Stenhouse.

Fletcher, R., Portalupi, J., & Williams, S. (2006). *When students write*. Portland, ME: Stenhouse. Video.

Flower, L., & Hayes, J. R. (2009). The cognition of discovery: Defining a rhetorical problem. In S. Miller (Ed.), *The Norton book of composition studies* (pp. 467–478). New York, NY: W. W. Norton. (Original work published 1980)

Flower, L., & Hayes, J. R. (1994). A cognitive process theory of writing. In R. B. Ruddell, M. R. Ruddell, & H. Singer (Eds.), *Theoretical models and processes of reading* (4th ed., pp. 928–950). Newark, DE: International Reading Association. (Original work published 1981)

Foley, G. (2008). *Don't worry bear*. New York, NY: Viking.

Fountas, I., & Pinnell, G. S. (2001). *Guiding readers and writers grades 3–6*. Portsmouth, NH: Heinemann.

Fu, D. (1995). *"My trouble is my English": Asian students and the American dream*. Portsmouth, NH: Heinemann.

Gardner, H. (1980). *Artful scribbles: The significance of children's drawings*. New York, NY: Basic Books.

Gee, J. (1996). *Social linguistics and literacies: Ideologies in discourses* (2nd ed.). Philadelphia, PA: RoutledgeFalmer.

Gersten, R., & Baker, S. (2001). Teaching expressive writing to students with learning disabilities: A meta-analysis. *The Elementary School Journal, 101*(3), 251–272.

Gillespie, P. Hughes, B. & Kail, H. (2007). Nothing marginal about this writing center experience: Using research about peer tutor alumni to educate others. In W. J. Macauley Jr. & N. Mauriello (Eds.), *Marginal words, marginal work? Tutoring the academy in the work of writing centers* (pp. 35–52). Cresskill, NJ: Hampton Press.

Goldstein, A., & Carr, P. G. (1996). Can students benefit from process writing? *NAEPfacts, 1*(3), Washington, DC: National Center for Education Statistics. Retrieved October 6, 2015, from nces.ed.gov/pubs96/web/96845.asp

Graham, S., & Hebert, M. (2011). Writing to read: A meta-analysis of the impact of writing and writing instruction on reading. *Harvard Educational Review, 81*(4), 710–785.

Graham, S., & Perin, D. (2007). *Writing next: Effective strategies to improve writing of adolescents in middle and high schools.* New York, NY: Alliance for Excellent Education.

Graves, D. (1982). A case study observing the development of primary children's composing, spelling, and motor behaviors during the writing process. Final Report. Durham, NH: New Hampshire University, Department of Education.

Graves, D. (2003). *Writing: Teachers and children at work.* Portsmouth, NH: Heinemann.

Graves, D., & Kittle, P. (2005). *My quick writes.* Portsmouth, NH: Heinemann.

Hale, E. (2008). *Crafting writers, K–6.* Portland, ME: Stenhouse Publishers.

Harris, M. (1992). Collaboration is not collaboration is not collaboration: Writing center tutorials vs. peer-response groups. *College Composition and Communication, 43*(3), 369–383.

Harris, M. (1995). Writing in the middle: Why writers need writing tutors. *College English, 57*(1), 27–42.

Harris, R. (1962). An experimental inquiry into the functions and value of formal grammar in the teaching of English, with special reference to the teaching of correct written English to children aged twelve to fourteen (Unpublished PhD dissertation). University of London.

Harvey, S. (1998). *Nonfiction matters: Reading, writing, and research in grades 3–8.* Portland, ME: Stenhouse.

Harvey, S., Goudvis, A., Muhtaris, K, & Ziemke, K. (2013). *Connecting comprehension and technology: Adapt and extend toolkit practices.* Portsmouth, NH: Heinemann.

Hayes, J. R. (2012). Modeling and remodeling writing. *Written Communication, 29*(3), 369–388.

Heard, G. (2003). *The revision toolbox: Teaching techniques that work.* Portsmouth, NH: Heinemann.

Heath, S. B. (1983). *Ways with words: Language, life, and work in communities and classrooms.* New York, NY: Cambridge University Press.

Hillocks, G., Jr. (1987). Synthesis of research on teaching writing. *Educational Leadership, 44*(8), 71–82.

Hillocks, G., Jr. (1995). *Teaching writing as reflective practice.* New York, NY: Teachers College Press.

IWCA. (2015, April 22). International Writing Centers Association position statement on secondary school writing centers. Retrieved from writingcenters.org/about/iwca-position-statements/

Karalitz, E. B. (1988). The rhythm of writing development. In T. Newkirk and N. Atwell (Eds.), *Understanding writing: Ways of observing, learning, and teaching K–8* (2nd ed., pp. 40–46). Portsmouth, NH: Heinemann.

Kent, R. (2010). *A guide to creating student-staffed writing centers.* New York: Peter Lang.

Kincaid, G. L. (1952). *Some factors affecting variations in the quality of students' writing* (Unpublished PhD dissertation). Boston University.

Lancia, P. J. (1997). Literary borrowing: The effects of literature on children's writing. *The Reading Teacher, 50,* 470–475.

Langer, J. A. (1986). *Children reading and writing: Structures and strategies.* Norwood, NJ: Ablex.

Law, I. (2008). *Savvy.* New York, NY: Dial.

Lerner, N. (2009). *The idea of a writing laboratory.* Carbondale, IL: Southern Illinois University Press.

Lindfors, J. (1999). *Children's Inquiry: Using language to make sense of the world.* New York, NY: Teachers College Press.

Lopez, M. E. (1999). *When discourses collide: An ethnography of migrant children at home and in school.* New York, NY: Peter Lang.

Lunsford, A. (1991). Collaboration, control, and the idea of a writing center. *Writing center Journal, 12*(1), 3–10.

Lyman, R. L. (1931, December). A co-operative experiment in junior high school composition. *School Review, 19,* 748–757.

Macrorie, K. (2009). Telling writing (4th ed.). In S. Miller (Ed.), *The Norton book of composition studies* (pp. 297–313). New York, NY: W. W. Norton. (Original work published 1985)

Marrin, A. (2006). *Oh, rats! The story of rats and people* (C. B. Mordan, Illus.). New York, NY: Dutton.

Meyer, E., & Smith, L. (1987). *The practical tutor.* New York, NY: Oxford.

Moll, L. C., Amanti, C., Neff, D., & Gonzalez, N. (1992). Funds of knowledge for teaching: Using a qualitative approach to connect homes and classrooms. *Theory into Practice, 31*(2), 132–141.

Murphy, C., & Law, J. (Eds.). (1995). *Landmark essays on writing centers.* Davis, CA: Hermagoras.

Murray, D. (1978a). Teaching the motivating force of revision. *The English Journal, 67*(7), 56–60.

Murray, D. (1978b). Write before writing. *College Composition and Communication, 29*(4), 375–381.

Murray, D. (1980). Writing as process: How writing finds its own meaning. In T. R. Donovan & B. W. McClelland (Eds.), *Eight approaches to teaching composition* (pp. 3–20). Urbana, IL: National Council of Teachers of English.

National Council of Teachers of English. (1985). *Resolution on grammar exercises to teach speaking and writing*. Retrieved from www.ncte.org/positions/statements/grammarexercises

National Governors Association Center for Best Practices & Council of Chief State School Officers. (2010) *Common Core State Standards*. Retrieved from www.corestandards.org

North, S. (1982, October). Training tutors to talk about writing. *College Composition and Communication, 35*, 300–311.

North, S. (1984). The idea of a writing center. *College English, 46*(5), 433–446.

Patrick, C. (1937). Creative thought in artists. *Journal of Psychology, 4*, 35–73.

Pearson, P. D., & Gallagher, M. C. (1983). The instruction of reading comprehension. *Contemporary Educational Psychology, 8*(3), 317–344.

Perl, S., & Egendorf, A. (1979). The process of creative discovery: Theory, research, and pedagogical implications. In D. McQuade (Ed.), *Linguistics, stylistics, and the teaching of composition* (pp. 118–134). Akron, OH: L & S Books.

Perl, S., & Schwartz, M. (2006). *Writing true: The art and craft of creative nonfiction*. Boston, MA: Houghton Mifflin.

Portalupi, J., & Fletcher, R. (2001). *Nonfiction craft lessons*. Portland, ME: Sten house.

Pritchard, R. J., & Honeycutt, R. L. (2006). The process approach to writing instruction: Examining its effectiveness. In C. A. MacArthur, S. Graham, & J. Fitzgerald (Eds.), *Handbook of Writing Research* (pp. 275–290). New York, NY: The Guilford Press.

Rafoth, B. (2015). *Multilingual writers and writing centers*. Boulder, CO: University of Boulder Press.

Rhodes, J. P. (2010). *Ninth ward*. New York, NY: Little, Brown Books for Young Readers.

Robinson, M. E. (1986). The writing performance and revision behavior of fifth grade process and non-process writing students during one-day and two-day writing sessions. *Dissertation Abstracts International, 49*(09A), 2536. (UMI No. AA18813469)

Routman, R. (2000). *Conversations*. Portsmouth, NH: Heinemann.

Routman, R. (2005). *Writing essentials*. Portsmouth, NH: Heinemann.

Rumelhart, D. E. (1981). Schemata: The building blocks of cognition. In J. T. Guthrie (Ed.), *Comprehension and teaching: Research reviews* (pp. 3–26). Newark, DE: International Reading Association.

Ryan, L., & Zimmerelli, L. (2010). *The Bedford guide for writing tutors*. New York: Bedford/St. Martin's.

Sanders, J., & Moudy, J. (2008). Literature apprentices: Understanding nonfiction text structures with mentor texts. *Journal of Children's Literature, 34*(2), 31–40.

Scardamalia, M., Bereiter, C., & Woodruff, E. (1980). *The effects of content knowledge on writing.* Paper presented at the Annual Meeting of the American Educational Research Association, Boston, MA.

Schön, D. A. (1984). *The reflective practitioner: How professionals think in action.* London, England: Basic Books.

Scollon, R., & Scollon, S. W. (1981). *Narrative, literacy, and face in interethnic communication.* Norwood, NJ: Ablex.

Scott , E. (2004). *Poles apart: Why penguins and polar bears will never be neighbors.* New York, NY: Viking Juvenile.

Shanahan, T., & Lomax, R. (1986). An analysis and comparison of theoretical models of the reading–writing relationship. *Journal of Educational Psychology, 78*(2), 116–123.

Shelton, N. R., & Fu, D. (2004). Creating a space for teaching writing and for test preparation. *Language Arts, 82*(2), 120–128.

Tardy, C., & Swales, J. (2008). Form, text organization, genre, coherence, and cohesion. In C. Bazerman (Ed.), *Handbook of research on writing: History, society, school, individual, text* (pp. 565–577). New York, NY: Lawrence Erlbaum Associates.

ten Have, P. (2007). *Doing conversation analysis: A practical guide.* Thousand Oaks, CA: SAGE.

Villanueva, V. (Ed.). (2003). *Cross-talk in comp theory* (2nd ed.). Urbana, IL: National Council of Teachers of English.

Vygotsky, L. S. (1978). *Mind in society.* Cambridge, MA: Harvard University Press.

Warlick, D. (2009). *Redefining literacy 2.0* (2nd ed.). Columbus, OH: Linworth.

Weaver, C. (1996). Teaching grammar in the context of writing. *English Journal, 85*(7), 15–24.

Wilcox, B. (1984, April). Conferencing tips. *Writing Lab Newsletter.* Urbana, IL: NCTE.

Wilcox, B., & Collins, N. D. (2003). Establishing and maintaining writing centers in middle, elementary, and preschool settings. In B. Silk (Ed.), *The writing center resource manual* (2nd ed., pp. 1–11). Emmitsburg, MD: NWCA Press.

Wilhelm, J. (2001). *Improving comprehension with think-aloud strategies.* New York, NY: Scholastic Professional Books.

Wood Ray, K. (1999). *Wondrous words: Writing and writers in the elementary classroom.* Urbana, IL: NCTE.

Wooffitt, R. (2005). *Conversation analysis and discourse analysis: A comparative and critical introduction.* Thousand Oaks, CA: SAGE.

Yolen, J. (1987). *Owl moon.* New York, NY: Philomel.

Zamel, V. (1982). The process of discovering meaning. *TESOL Quarterly, 16*(2), 195–209.

Zumbrunn, S., & Krause, K. (2012). Conversations with leaders: Principles of effective writing instruction. *The Reading Teacher, 65*(5), 346–353.

Index

About the Authors

Jennifer Sanders received her PhD in 2006 from the University of Florida in curriculum and instruction with a specialization in language, literacy, and culture. She is currently an associate professor of literacy education in the College of Education at Oklahoma State University and specializes in K–12 writing instruction. Jennifer has been a member of the OSU Writing Project for 9 years and completed the Summer Institute in 2015. Her academic passions are developing teachers' knowledge of effective writing instruction and supporting the literacy learning of underserved students in high-needs communities. Her interest in high-needs educational settings stems from experience teaching in rural, high-poverty schools in Florida and working with urban schools in Oklahoma and Belize. Her research interests include writing and writing center pedagogy, writing-teacher education, teacher professional development, and representations of multiculturalism in children's literature. Jennifer's work in multicultural children's literature includes service as former chair of the Notable Books for a Global Society 2013 awards. Her previous work on the relationship between artistic and written composing processes of children is presented in her co-edited book titled *Literacies, the Arts, and Multimodality*.

Rebecca L. Damron received her PhD in 1997 from Oklahoma State University in English with a specialization in applied linguistics. She taught at the University of Tulsa for 5 years, directing the Writing Program and Writing Center for 2 of those years. As an English professor in the Rhetoric and Professional Writing Program at Oklahoma State University, she directed the OSU Writing Center for 10 years. Under her tenure, the writing center developed a robust community outreach mission that included supervising the development of a writing center at the local high school, as well as collaborating with the local children's museum, domestic violence shelter, and library to engage in writing activities. Rebecca is the co-author of *How Architects Write*, published by Routledge. Rebecca also served as the OSU Writing Project director for 3 years and was a site member for several years before that, working intimately with teachers across the state to improve their writing pedagogy.

Printed and bound by CPI Group (UK) Ltd, Croydon, CR0 4YY

09/06/2025

14685968-0002